Principals of Property Law

Law School Notes 2018

FitchLaw, Inc.

Copyright:
Copyright 2018 FitchLaw. All rights reserved. No part of this publication may be stored in a retrieval system, transmitted, or reproduced in any way, including but not limited to photocopy, photographs, magnetic, or other record, without the prior agreement and written permission of the publisher.

The author and publisher have made their best efforts to prepare this book. The author and publisher make no representation or warranties of any kind with regards to the completeness or accuracy of the contents herein and accepts no liability of any kind, including but not limited to performance, merchantability, fitness for any particular purpose or any losses or damages of any kind caused or alleged to be caused directly or indirectly from this book.

Trademarks:
FitchLaw Inc., has attempted throughout this book to distinguish proprietary trademarks from descriptive terms by following the capitalization style used by the manufacturer.
Published by: FitchLaw Inc.

FitchLaw Inc., welcome corrections and comments on its documents. In addition to comments, please send comments on typographical, formatting, or other errors. Simply make a copy of the relevant page, mark the error, and send it to fitchlawupdates@gmail.com. Books and testing materials are available at special quantity discounts to use as premiums and sales promotions, or for corporate training programs, as well as other educational programs.

Printed in the United States of America. No part of this work may be reproduced or transmitted in any form or by any means, electronic, manual, photocopying, recording, or by any information storage and retrieval systems, without prior written permission of the publisher.

ISBN-13: 978-1986236799 (paperback)

PROPERTY OUTLINE

I: What Is Property? Two Conceptions of Property

The two main conceptions of property are: <u>Property as a right to a thing good against all the world</u>, and the contrasting conception of <u>property as a collection, or "bundle," of rights, with content that varies according to context and policy choices.</u>

RIGHT TO EXCLUDE

- ***Jacques v. Steenberg Homes, Inc.:*** Court upheld the right of the plaintiffs to exclude the defendants from their property. The right to exclude means that one cannot enter onto another's land without the consent of the owner.
    - The court emphasized that the right to exclude was one of the most *"essential sticks on the bundle of rights that are commonly characterized as property."*
    - <u>Given rationale for enforcement of the right to exclude:</u> (1) Enforcing the right to exclude means that landowners are less likely to resort to "self-help" measures, and (2) Protection of the right to privacy.
        - The court did not explain why these rights were included in private property.
    - <u>The court held that, even though Steenberg did not damage the plaintiffs' property, they were entitled to damages.</u>

- Main justifications for the right to exclude:
    - <u>(1)</u>: Private property is necessary to avoid the tragedy of the commons and incentivize investment in improvements.
        - **Counter:** Not applicable if there is no commons (e.g. this does not apply in the Steenberg case above).
    - <u>(2)</u>: It is good to have individual owners make decisions of how land is to be used because they are closer to the resources that will be used. It is better to decentralize the decision-making than it is to centralize it.
        - **Counter:** Centralization allows for large-scale coordination between many different owners (e.g. regional urban planning); can lead to economies of scale.
    - <u>(3)</u>: The right to exclude is not the end, but rather is a means to an end in that it protects our interest in using things. Protecting one's interest in using things allows for personal autonomy. Thus, we can justify the right to exclude as a way of protecting individual autonomy.
        - **Counter:** Unlimited right to exclude can lead to societally-suboptimal outcomes, e.g. racial covenants like in *Shelley.*
    - <u>(4)</u>: The Lockean idea that we want to reward people for their labor. This has an economic component, in that the right to exclude means that only the landowner who put the effort into improving the land or using it for economic activity can reap the fruits of his labor, and also a moral component (the expenditure of labor has a kind of moral value which we reward by allowing the laborer to keep the fruits of his labor).

- Why a clear rule (rather than case-by-case standard)?
    - People need to have predictability regarding what will happen when they take a certain action (lower bargaining and transaction costs).
    - Right to exclude so fundamentally important that we will enforce it even when it seems irrational.

- *Hinman v. Pacific Air Transport:* Court rejected application of *ad coelum* doctrine to airspace above piece of land (thus negating trespass claim); holding instead that the owner of land owns as much of the space above him as he uses, but only so long as he uses it (i.e. only the airspace to which the owner is exercising dominion). Everything else in the space above is public.
    - *Ad coelum doctrine:* Whomever owns a piece of land owns all the airspace above the property, and also owns the depths below the property.
        - The court's rationale for rejecting the doctrine was in part that it had been invented long before the existence of airplanes, and that the doctrine had never been taken literally.
        - The *ad coelum* rule is fundamental to property in land – deeds to land are always stated in terms of some measurement of the surface area. Absent zoning restrictions or covenant, the ad coelum rule allows the owner of the surface to construct a building as tall as engineering permits.
    - The court held that Hinman could recover damages only if the "trespass" of the planes into the airspace above his house resulted in some sort of injury (if they interfered with the use of the land).
    - Issues with *Ad Coelum*:
        - **Tragedy of the anticommons**
            - Granting landowners a right to sue overflying airplanes for trespass would lead to serious transaction cost issues for the airlines (who would have to negotiate with each landowner affected by airplane flights); would severely retard development of air travel.

CONCEPTS OF PROPERTY – PHILOSOPHICAL PERSPECTIVES
- Two general tendencies – <u>**essentialists**</u> (who attempt to uncover the single true definition of property as legal concept); <u>**Skeptics**</u> (who believe that it is fruitless to try and come up with a single canonical conception of what property means in a legal system). The skeptical view is reflected in the idea of a <u>**"bundle of rights"**</u>. This second view is reflected in the Restatement of Property.
    - Essentialism is currently making something of a comeback.
- Penner: *The Idea of Property in Law*. Property is a *"right in rem"*, contrasted with a *"right in personam."*
    - Rights *in rem* are normative – they have nothing to do with any particular individual's personality. They are good against all the world, regardless of who holds them.
    - **Exclusion thesis:** The right to property is a right to exclude others from things which is grounded by the interest we have in the use of things.

- **In rem right:** An in rem right creates duties in a large and indefinite class of others ("all the world").
- **In personam right:** A right which creates a duty in only a small and definitely ascertained # of others.
    - Very roughly, the law of torts as applied to persons and the core of the law of property establish *in rem* rights, while the law of contract establishes *in personam* rights.
    - In rem rights tend to be simple, easily understood duties of noninterference (e.g. "no hitting" or "no trespassing"). Complicated rights that impose affirmative duties to take particular actions are more likely to be in personam and hence will be more likely to be imposed by contract or govt. regulations.
- **Tom Grey:** *The Disintegration of Property.* Upholds the "bundle of rights" conception of property. Notes that this has political implications (if property is a bundle of rights, then it can be subject to the government's will – e.g. bans on racial covenants).

NUISANCE (OVERVIEW/COASE THEOREM)

Hendricks v. Stalmaker: Defendant drilled a water well within 100 feet of the drainage field of plaintiffs' proposed septic system; plaintiffs were refused a permit to build it. Plaintiffs argued that well was a nuisance because it interfered with their property rights by precluding their installation of a septic system on their property. Court held that there was no nuisance, and that the **balance of interests** weighed in favor of the well because the leach field was more invasive and damaging to defendant than well was to plaintiff.

- **Private Nuisance defined:** "A substantial and unreasonable interference with the private use and enjoyment of another's land." Recovery for a private nuisance is limited to plaintiffs who have suffered a significant harm to their property rights or privileges caused by the interference.
    - Nuisance actions are *ad personam* rather than *ad rem*.
- **Distinction between trespass and nuisance:** Trespass protects interests in **possession** of the land, while nuisance protects the **use and enjoyment** of the land. Trespass applies when intrusion is with some large and solid object enough to physically displace the plaintiff.
    - The two standards exemplify two different strategies for resolving disputes about how scarce resources are used: **exclusion and governance**.
        - **Exclusion:** Decisions about resource use delegated to an owner who acts as the manager or gatekeeper of the resource (e.g. owner gets to decide who comes onto the land).
            - **Trespass reflects an exclusion strategy.**
        - **Governance:** Focuses on particular uses of resources and prescribes particular rules about permitted and prohibited uses without regard to the other attributes of the resource.
            - **Law of nuisance reflects a governance strategy.**

THE COASE THEOREM

- <u>In a world with 0 transaction costs</u>, economically efficient outcome will occur regardless of which party has the legal entitlement.
- <u>In a world with transaction costs > 0</u>, legal entitlement should be placed where it will minimize costs.
- **Other assumptions:** Individuals are rational maximizers and that all values are capable of being expressed in monetary terms.

RESOLVING PROPERTY DISPUTES BY CONTRACT
- Contractual modifications of property rights (**"Coasean bargains"**) should be explored as alternative to litigation.
- **Why don't Coasean solutions happen? (1)** Parties don't think about these kinds of solutions; **(2)** Parties thought about them, but concluded that they were too costly or infeasible; **(3)** Parties did not think about them until transaction costs became too high for any kind of Coasean bargain to take place.
- **Assembly problems:** Arise when someone wants to assemble property rights from a large number of owners in order to undertake some project.
    - High transaction costs stem from the fact that there are large numbers of contracting parties (difficulties in identifying the owners and getting them to agree).
    - Some owners might be holdouts for very generous payments.
- **Bilateral monopoly:** Situations in which one owner of property needs something that can be provided by only one other person or entity.
    - Also source of high transaction costs because each of the parties has nowhere else to turn in order to engage in an equivalent transaction.

REPEATED TRESPASS
- *Baker v. Howard County Hunt (Maryland 1936):* Baker did rabbit experiments on farm. Hunt club held hunts with bloodhounds in the vicinity of the farm. Dogs attacked rabbits and injured Baker's wife. Hunt sent letter of apology but made no efforts to keep the dogs off of the land. In 1936, Baker shot dogs to get them off his property. Baker sought injunction to keep hunt club from hunting on his land.
    - **Holding:** Equity could afford injunctive relief against trespasses which, while not continuous, are nevertheless part of a single course of conduct that seriously interferes with the right of a landowner to the peaceful enjoyment of his property.
        - Hunters are trespassers if on another's land.
        - Owner of a dog is not liable for dog's trespass on land of its own volition, **but** is liable if the owner knows that the dog, due to nature, training, and instinct, will probably damage the property of others, or if with that knowledge he permits it to stray beyond its control.
    - **Clean hands:** Hunt club argued that Baker not entitled to equitable relief because <u>(1)</u> Adequate remedy at law, and <u>(2)</u> Baker did not come into equity with clean hands since he shot at dogs.
        - No adequate remedy at law because it was not possible to monetarily value the loss to Baker's experiments (experiments were a **unique good**).

- Baker did not develop unclean hands by shooting the dogs, since they were attacking his wife and his chickens.
    - **Note 1:** The two main maxims of equity are **(1)** That he who comes into equity must come with clean hands; **(2)** Equitable remedies only available when the law is inadequate.

BUILDING ENCROACHMENTS
- *Pile v. Pedrick (Penn. 1895):* Foundation of defendant's building partially encroached on plaintiff's land; encroachment was very small (1 ⅜ inches). Trial judge directed that the defendants had to remove their wall. Defendants appealed in part because the plaintiffs were not willing to permit the defendants to enter onto their land and chip off the offending ends of the wall.
    - **Holding:** Plaintiffs were under no obligation to allow the defendants to enter onto plaintiffs' land to chip off the wall.
        - Even though trespass was small, plaintiffs were under no obligation to allow the defendants to enter onto their land.
        - Court affirmed the right to exclude even though the trespass was made in good faith (based upon a mistaken survey).
        - Decision has a greater *ex ante* effect, but could incentivize investing too much in surveying costs.
- *Golden Press v. Rylands (Col. 1951):* West wall of appellant's (Golden Press's) building protruded between two inches and 3.5 inches onto appellee's (Rylands's) land. **Mistake was in good faith.** Plaintiffs sought an injunction requiring that the defendant remove all footings and foundations on their property.
    - **Holding:** Court did not grant injunction, but allowed Rylands to seek a remedy in law for damages.
    - If encroachment is deliberate (i.e. in bad faith), and constitutes a willful taking of another's land, equity may require restoration regardless of the expense of removal.
        - **However**, if encroachment is in **good faith**, then the court should **weigh the circumstances so as to not act oppressively**.
    - If hardship is disproportionate then injunction won't be awarded – only damages.
    - Furthermore, encroachment was *de minimis*
    - **Rationale:** Both plaintiff and defendant had clean hands/didn't intend the trespass.
        - Avoids social waste – **expense and hardship of removal much greater in comparison with any advantage of the plaintiffs to be gained thereby.**
- **Note 2:** Safe generalization today would be that, if faced with the facts of *Pile* or *Golden Press* (unintentional encroachment, slight damages to plaintiff's interest, grave hardship to the defendant if removal of the encroachment were required) – most American courts today would probably deny injunctive relief and award only damages.
- **Note 3:** Once true state of affairs was revealed, the encroacher knew that it had placed an unwanted structure on someone else's land. From that point onward, the continuing presence of the encroaching structure is an **intentional trespass.**

- **Note 4:** Maxim of equity is that injunction will be issued if a weighing of the interests between the parties – "**balance of the equities**" – favors giving the victorious plaintiff the "extraordinary" relief of an injunction.
- **Note 5:** Courts employ the balancing of the equities approach to deny injunctions against building encroachments **only when the original encroachment is innocent** – i.e. when the encroaching party was acting in good faith.
  - For bad faith violations, courts universally agree that injunctive relief is appropriate.
- **Note 6 – Four factor test:** In the context of IP rights (specifically patents), SCOTUS embraced the *Golden Press* position on the issue. Patent holder must satisfy a four-part test:
  - **(1)** Patent holder suffered an irreparable injury.
  - **(2)** Remedies available at law are inadequate to compensate for that injury.
  - **(3)** Considering balance of hardships between plaintiff and defendant, an equitable remedy is warranted.
  - **(4)** Public interest would not be disserved by a permanent injunction.

EX ANTE/EX POST PROBLEM
- **Ex ante** – refers to an analysis of the situation before some critical event (e.g. contract) takes place.
- **Ex post** – Refers to an analysis of the situation after such a critical event occurs.
- In context of building encroachment, **ex ante analysis** would consider the circumstances of two adjacent landowners before the building is constructed, while **ex post analysis** would consider the circumstances of the two landowners after the building is constructed.
- Courts generally drawn to ex post analysis because this is how controversies are presented to them.

II: How Do You Acquire Property (Other Than By Gift or Purchase)?

A: First Possession
- *Pierson v. Post:* Respondent had been hunting a fox with dogs (on publicly-owned land), and was in hot pursuit when the appellant popped up, shot it, and carried it off. The court found in favor of Pierson, holding that post had not done enough to establish possession of the fox – **he had only been in pursuit without wounding the animal.**
  - **Majority:** Title to a wild animal requires *certain control* (either capture of the wild animal or something close to capture, e.g. having mortally wounded the animal and still being in pursuit).
    - **Policy Rationale:** The imposition of such a rule would reduce disputes and therefore reduce litigation. When the next dispute about a fox comes up, there would be (hopefully) no litigation.
  - **Dissent:** To establish possession, one would have to be in pursuit and have some reasonable prospect of catching the animal. However, this is far less than certain control.

- - - **Policy Rationale:** The dissent thought that there would not be any incentive to go out and exterminate this particular form of vermin if others were allowed to *free ride on the labor of others (flushing out and pursuing the animal)*.
      - The dissent therefore put weight on desert arising from the expenditure of labor.
    - The dissent thought that *custom* among the hunters should have been allowed to decide this case (the hunters would be able to sort this out).s
  - The impact of the rule may depend on the reasons why people go hunting for foxes. If it is the spirit of the hunt which is motivating the killing, then the sort of property right may not matter.
- <u>A first in time rule can lead to wasteful competitions and races to be first. First-in-time seems to work best when a clear winner will emerge quickly because of that person's special skill or relation to the resource.</u>
- ***Ghen v. Rich:*** The libellant (plaintiff) was a whaler, who shot and killed a whale with a bomb-lance. The whale sunk, washed ashore, and was found by someone who sold the whale at auction to the respondent, who shipped off the blubber and tried out the oil. The court found in favor of the libellant.
  - **Rationale:** The court's decision relied on an **industry custom** that the person who kills a whale in the above manner owns it (the finder of the whale on the beach would receive a finder's fee). The court theorized that, without this rule, <u>no person would engage in the business of whaling if the "fruits of his labor" could be appropriated by any chance finder.</u>
  - **The finder's argument** probably relied in part on the idea brought forth in *Pierson v. Post*, namely that possession requires control. In regards to the custom argument, the finder could have argued that custom is not dispositive, and thus does not control in this case (especially since there was no evidence that the finder was a member of the whaling community).
  - **The whaler's argument:** Also rooted in *Pierson v. Post* (he mortally wounded the whale), and also based in custom (the shooter has legal possession of the whale).
  - **Policy Considerations:** The goal was to encourage the hunting of whales, and this rule incentivizes hunting by assuring whalers that the fruits of their labor would be rewarded.
    - Industry custom could lead to collusion between industry players with a monopoly to collude to exclude actors trying to enter the industry.
- ***Keeble v. Hickeringill:*** Hickeringill fires gun to scare away ducks on neighbor's property. It's unclear whether Keeble had any control over the ducks
  - Hickeringill's bad faith makes this an easier case for the court.
  - Court also rules for Keeble because he has right to things on his land, which Hickeringill disturbed.

Elinor Ostrom: *Governing the Commons*
- **Tragedy of the Commons:** If a resource is open to all to exploit – i.e. "a commons" (rather than privatized and parceled out), then a rational economic actor will exploit the resource to the best of his abilities. This is because he derives the direct benefit of his labor (e.g. fishing

in the sea, grazing cattle on a commons), and suffers only delayed costs from the deterioration of the commons, which he and others collectively overexploit.
- **The result of this system is the long-term destruction and ruin of the commons.**
- This result is supported empirically by modern resource economics, which have concluded that, where a number of users have access to a common-pool resource, the total # of resource units withdrawn from the resource will be greater than the optimal economic level of withdrawal.
- **Policy Proscriptions:** (1) Leviathan as the only way; (2) Privatization as the only way; (3) Prof. Ostrom's "alternative solution."
    - **Leviathan:** To avoid the tragedy of the commons, an external force (i.e. the government) must exert control over natural resource systems through an agency.
        - **Problem:** the optimal equilibrium of resource use can only be reached if the central agency has valid and reliable information concerning the resource and the actors exploiting it. Without this information, a central agency can make serious errors.
    - **Privatization:** The only way to avoid the tragedy of the commons is to impose private property rights whenever resources are owned in commons.
        - **Problem** (at least in how it is presented theoretically): It assumes the commons is perfectly homogenous throughout, and thus can be divided into equal shares.
            - This is not true – sometimes the resource being exploited consists of wild animals (e.g. fish) which flow between parcels of land, and in other cases the resource simply is not homogenous. Parcelizing the commons might therefore be impossible (or at least impossible to do equitably).
            - Additionally, the private owners might have imperfect information themselves.
    - **The alternative solution:** Effectively a form of voluntarist corporatism. Prof. Ostrom proposed that the exploiters of a commons (her example was herders in a commonly-owned meadow) make a binding contract to commit themselves to a cooperative strategy that they themselves work out.
        - **Problem:** Information problems as before, the possibility of the breakdown of the internal monitoring system, the inability of the external enforcer to enforce *ex post*.
    - **The "empirical alternative":** A distributist system which a village in Turkey adopted to parcel out the rights to fish in a local lake. The fishery's economic viability had been threatened by unrestrained use of the fishery (which led to hostility between fishermen), and competition among fishers for the better fishing spots which led to increased production costs. The system which the fishers adopted parceled out the best fishing spots by lot, and called for each fisher to cycle through all the fishing spots, so that each individual boat got the opportunity to fish in a spot frequented by migrating fish. This system led to an optimization of the site's production capabilities, and a reduction in resource waste (no more searching for or fighting over a site).

Commons, Anticommons, and Semicommons
- **Tragedy of the Commons:** As described above in the Ostrom section.

- **Tragedy of the Anticommons:** The idea that if too many people hold rights in a piece of property, and thus if too many permissions are required to exploit a resource, then rights to the larger resource may never be assembled. This is because
    - (1) the transaction costs are too high
    - (2) Some rightsholders might act as "holdouts" (people who hold out for a better price) or
    - (3) They might act irrationally and refuse to grant permission to use their share of the resources.
- **For both Tragedies**:
    - An individual has an incentive to act in a way that imposes costs on others, either by exercising her right of access (to a commons) or her right to exclude others (to an anticommons).
    - Overcoming the problem requires some kind of realignment of rights, and doing this requires dealing with holdouts and freeriders.
- **Tragedy of the *Semicommons*:** This occurs when a given resource is subject to private exclusion rights in some uses or along some dimensions, but is a commons or open access for other purposes or along other dimensions.

Individual Transferable Quotas (ITQs) and The Destruction of Ocean Fisheries

- Transferable permits share some of the attributes associated with property, such as conferring widely dispersed authority, having monetary value, and being alienable. <u>In traditional property terms, transferable permits are closer to licenses rather than in rem rights.</u>
- Jonathan Adler, *Legal Obstacles to Private Ordering in Marine Fisheries* (2002)
    - Conservation of marine fisheries presents the archetypical "commons" problem – so long as there is open access to the fishery, each fisher has an incentive to catch as much as possible, even beyond the point of sustainability.
    - Creation of property rights is the most obvious means of preventing the tragedy of the commons.
        - As a general rule, when resources are owned, there is less concern about their overuse.
        - Existence of externalities is often attributable to the absence of property rights and the consequent rights to contract.
    - Various legal doctrines (including **public trust doctrine**) hold that fisheries are held in trust by the gov't for the common use of all citizens. Most fishery conservation efforts rely upon gov't regulation.
        - Traditional regulatory approaches (e.g. limits on fishing seasons, boat size, fishing areas) have been <u>a spectacular failure</u>.
            - Measures are inefficient because they are all indirect means of conserving fish stocks.
            - Result: Overcapitalization in fisheries and **destructive racing behavior.**
    - ITQs: Government sets the total allowable catch for a given season, and then allocates shares of the catch – a quota – to individuals, boats and firms as a form of **transferable right**.

- ITQ programs have been implemented in several countries, with substantial success at increasing fishing efficiency, reducing overcapitalization, and lessening the ecological impact of fishing operations.
  - <u>Most importantly,</u> ITQs have encouraged fishers to exercise greater stewardship.
- ITQs have been implemented in U.S. fisheries, but there has been a moratorium since 1996.
  - Monitoring and tracking devices (e.g. branding and fencing) are emerging in the marine context.
  - **Fisher co-operatives:** Alternative to ITQs whereby the main fishing companies cooperate to increase efficiency.
    - <u>Helps reduce overcapitalization, inefficiency, and waste.</u>
    - <u>Decreases racing behavior.</u>
  - Experience with marine resources suggests that environmental problems are more the result of government failure – we have failed to have effective private institutions, and government policy is sometimes the cause.
- *Alliance against IFQs v. Brown (9th Cir.)*: Issue in this case was whether regulations for implementing a fishery management plan were arbitrary and capricious, or violative of the authorizing statute.
  - **Holding:** Regulations were a permissible exercise of authority by the Secretary of Commerce.
  - **Rationale:** Court noted that the IFQ scheme had the practical effect of transferring economic power over the fishery from those who fished to those who owned or leased fishing boats (more powerful institutional actors).
    - If participation in the fishery while the rule was under consideration had been considered, then people would have fished and invested in boats in order to obtain quota shares
      - <u>This would have exacerbated overcapacity and made no economic sense (wasteful racing behavior).</u>
        - Because of this, rule was not arbitrary and capricious.
- Katrina Wyman, *From Fur to Fish: Reconsidering the Evolution of Private Property (2005)*:
  - <u>Three waves of ocean enclosures:</u>
    - <u>(1)</u> Coastal countries began creating national property rights in parts of the oceans that were historically commons. 1982 Convention on the Laws of the Sea codified this
    - <u>(2)</u> Countries domestically began subdividing their expanded national rights over the oceans into communal regimes at the regional level.
      - In many fisheries, establishment of a collective regime was followed by the creation of even smaller scale, species-specific communal regimes.
    - <u>(3)</u> [Potential] third wave of enclosure would create <u>individual property rights out of communal or national regimes (ITQs)</u>. This wave has been stalled

- **Reasons for why ITQs are not widespread:** Institutional actors (Department of Commerce, federal courts, members of Congress) may block recommendations to establish ITQs for political/judicial reasons.
- Two main reasons stand out why tradable rights have been slow to develop in coastal fisheries in federal waters:
    - **(1)** Political institutions through which tradable rights are established provide for multiple veto points for interest groups to delay the pace of change.
    - **(2)** Existence of conflicts among fishing interest groups over how to allocate the increased rents that tradable rights are expected to generate.

Other Applications of First Possession
- **Abandoned or lost property** is subject to the rule of first possession.
    - If property is abandoned, the first person to find it can claim it.
    - If property is lost, the finder has a superior right to the property relative to everyone in the world except for the true owner.
- **Sunken Vessels:** Possession of sunken vessels gives rise to rights under the law of finds, or to rights of salvage under the law of salvage. The law of maritime finds awarded ownership to the first possessor, but only if the vessel was abandoned (and not still claimed by its owners or their insurers), and therefore unowned at the time of taking possession.
    - If the vessel is not abandoned, a successful "salvor" has a claim for a generous percentage of the value of the vessel and its cargo, but does not acquire ownership of the vessel or its full value. Acts that are sufficient for salvage-possession might not be sufficient for a finder to establish acquisition-possession. **To enjoy a right to exclusive possession and protection from interference of rival salvors, a salvor must exercise due diligence and must be capable of actually saving the property.**
    - Since the original owners lose rights if a vessel is deemed abandoned, courts tend to favor applying the law of salvage rather than the law of finds in ambiguous situations.
- **Treasure Trove:** For gold and silver in any form hidden for later discovery (other than as unmined minerals in place), the law of treasure trove may apply. Treasure trove applies to caches of gold and silver and sometimes other valuables on land or sea.
    - Abandoned Shipwreck Act - "qualifying shipwrecks in navigable waters are subject to federal ownership, immediately transferred to the state in which the wreck is located."
- **The Baseball Case (*Popov v. Hayashi*):** Baseballs used in professional games are considered to be the property of the home team, but once they leave the playing field they are regarded as abandoned property. Here, Popov had at least partial control over a ball before it was knocked out of his hands in a brawl (**he had a "pre-possessory interest" in the ball, according to the judge**), and then Hayashi, who was uninvolved in the brawl, captured it entirely. The court awarded both parties an equal and undivided interest in the ball – forcing them to auction off the baseball.
    - Is this what both parties wanted? Maybe one person valued the ball beyond its economic value and this rule resulted in a loss to them?

- **Oil and Gas:** Under common law, oil and gas are subject to the **rule of capture** – an application of first possession.
    - **Rule of Capture:** Surface owners are free to pump oil and gas from the surface of their parcels, as long as the drilling apparatus stays within the "column of space" projected down from the surface.
    - "Slant drilling" (drilling at an angle that intersects a neighbor's column of space) is a form of trespass.
    - If no curbs placed on pumping, then **a tragedy of the commons results**.
        - Pumping will be too rapid (**racing behavior**), thereby wasting the natural propulsion from gas located around the oil. The race to pump would also lead to greater surface storage of oil.
    - **Solution:** Have each owner take shares in a field under **unitary management**. Some statutes provide for compulsory unitization upon a vote by some supermajority of the owners over a field.
    - Oil and gas often referred to as "fugacious" or "fugitive minerals", and are analogized to wild animals.
- *Garza:* Question of whether subsurface fracking could give rise to an action in trespass.
    - **Holding:** No – Rule of capture means that subsurface minerals belong to whomever gets to them first.

B: DISCOVERY

Whereas first possession requires that one be the first **actually to possess** an unclaimed thing, discovery establishes a unique **right to possess** a thing.

- *Johnson v. M'Intosh*: Plaintiffs were the heirs of people who had purchased land from the Piankeshaw Indians prior to 1795. In 1795, the Illinois and Piankeshaw Indians had entered into treaties with the US, retaining certain lands as reservations, but ceding to the federal government other of the lands they had previously occupied. The US sold to the defendant some of the same lands granted to the plaintiffs.
    - **The principle of discovery:** Per an agreement between the European powers, discovery gave title to the government by whose subjects, or by whose authority, the discovery had occurred, against all other European governments, whose title might be consummated by possession.
        - The exclusion of all other Europeans gave to the nation making the discovery the sole right of acquiring the soil from the natives. This right could be ceded to other European powers in peace treaties.
    - **Native title:** The natives had only a right of occupancy to the land, and the exclusive power to extinguish this right was vested in the government (here, the US federal government) which had the right to acquire the territories. US-granted titles thus trumped Indian-granted or derived titles.
    - **Rationales/Policy Arguments:**
        - (1) The right of conquest (if a country conquered the tribes, then they could dispose of the conquered lands as they wished)

- **(2)** The fact that the extinguishing of native title was a *fait accompli* in the entire eastern half of the United States at the time, and to recognize native title would therefore call a whole bunch of land deeds into question.
      - **(3)** Property rights extend from power (power to hold the property against all takers). POWER is central to property rights, and the granting of property rights.
  - **"Chains of title"**: When faced with competing claims to a single piece of property, courts recreate the "chains of title", underlying the competing claims, in order to determine which of the parties had the stronger claim. Each claim is traced back a link at a time, until we arrive at the "root of title." Often, this exercise will lead back to a single common grantor (e.g. the government or the first possessor), in which cases the first transferee from the common granter is deemed to have the better claim to title.
      - Marshall drew a distinction between sovereign title ("dominion") based on discovery, and Indian title ("occupancy") based on possession. He then traces the chain of title back in time, looking to acts of discovery to establish dominion rather than occupancy.

C: BY CREATION

- Property right? Without property protection one disincentivizes the gathering of information (nobody wants to put the effort in to gather information if there is no protection), but increases innovation.
    - On the other hand, having property rights prevents innovation (can't freely use ideas of others) but incentivizes the gathering of information
- ***Int'l News Service v. Associated Press***: INS took news reports of AP's and put them in their newspapers. AP claimed unfair competition, and sought to restrain the pirating of their news.
  - Questions:
      - **(1)** Whether there is any property in news;
      - **(2)** If there is property in news, does it survive the instance of its publication in the first newspaper to which it is communicated by the news-gatherer, and
      - **(3)** Did INS's admitted course of conduct in appropriating for commercial use matter taken from AP publications constitute unfair competition in trade?
  - Holding: Court recognized a **"quasi-property right** in the news; right only recognizable against INS (in personam).
      - Justifications
        - **Commercial:** Also restricted in time to when the news only has a commercial value to AP.
        - **Lockean:** Court grants it because of a "reap where you did not sow" argument.
            - **Counter:** news is a public good and it might be beneficial to society at large to let anyone distribute it.
        - **Custom:** INS also breached the custom but they had a reason because their news cables were cut in Europe because of their coverage of the war angered their governments.

THE RIGHT OF PUBLICITY
- *Midler v. Ford Motor Co.*: Bette Midler sued Ford for hiring someone to sing her signature song – and trying to closely imitate Midler's voice – in a car commercial.
  - Neither Midler's name nor her picture was used in the commercial, and Ford's ad agency had a license from the copyright holder to use the song.
  - **Holding:** Celebrities have a <u>right of publicity</u>, which they can sell. Midler's right of publicity was appropriated by Ford, and thus Ford committed a tort.
    - Court noted that what Ford sought was an attribute of Midler's identity, valued at what the market would have paid for Midler to have sung the commercial in person.
    - **Justifications for holding:**
      - "Reaping w/o sowing" – Ford was reaping the rewards of being associated with Midler's identity without actually providing some sort of remuneration to her.
      - **Incentive argument:** No incentive to develop a persona or invest in vocal training if others can reap what Midler has sown.
    - **Concerns:**
      - Is a person's voice equivalent to their identity?
- The *Vanna White* Case: Advertisement contained image of a robot in a dress turning letters on a board made up to resemble the one in the television show. White sued for violation of her right of publicity.
  - **Holding:** Court upheld White's common law right to publicity.
  - **Dissent (Kozinski):** Argued that this was a ludicrous extension of the right of publicity. Kozinski stressed the need for IP law to strike balances between what is set aside for the owner and what is left in the public domain (e.g. parody, fair use, idea-expression dichotomy).
    - In effect, <u>per this ruling, every famous person now has an exclusive right to anything that reminds the viewer of her.</u>
    - It is the Wheel of Fortune set, not the robot's attributes, that evoke White's image.

NOVELTY
- *Trenton Industries v. A.E. Peterson Manufacturing Co*: Complaint alleged infringement of a patent (on a new style of folding high chair), and the recovery of compensation for the use of the patented device during the period prior to the patent's issuance.
  - **Holding:** Court held that the supposed advance in high chair technology did not warrant the issuance of a patent, but that the defendant owed compensation for appropriating the new idea and using it as a template for its own foldable high chairs.
    - **Patent:** At the time, for a patent to be issued, an idea needed to be a novel improvement (a nonobvious improvement) rather than an improvement which is the product of mechanical skill (a small improvement). The folding high chair improvement which had been patented here was in the latter category.

- **Stealing the idea:** Lack of a patent aside, if a person communicates a novel idea to another with the intention that the latter may use the idea and compensate that person for the use, the other party must pay compensation if he appropriates the idea.
    - **Note 3:** In copyright law, the corresponding "newness" requirement is "originality".

D: BY ACCESSION

- **Principle of Accession:** This refers to a family of doctrines, each of which shares a common feature: <u>ownership of some unclaimed or contested resource is assigned to the owner of some *other* resource that has a particularly prominent relationship to the unclaimed or contested resource.</u>
- **Doctrine of Accession:** This refers to a narrower common-law doctrine that is part of this larger family of doctrines.
    - This doctrine applies when someone mistakenly tales up a physical object that belongs to someone else and transforms it through her labor into a fundamentally different object.

Increase

- The general rule is that the offspring or increase of tame or domestic animals belongs to the owner of the dam or mother.
    - Furthermore, the increase of the increase, ad infinitum, of domestic animals comes within the rule and belongs to the owner of the original stock.
    - This is a rule, not a standard – courts have not carved out exceptions for calves sired by prize-winning bulls, for example, or for calves raised at great expense by someone other than the mother. One exception in English law was for cygnets or baby swans.

Accession

- *Wetherbee v. Green:* Defendant cut timber on land owned by defendant, and used the timber to create barrel-hoops. Defendant cut the timber in good faith (he thought that he had the right to use the trees).
    - **Holding:** The defendant had the right to show to the jury that he had manufactured the hoops in good faith, and in the belief that he had the proper authority to do so.
        - **If he succeeded in making these showings**, he was entitled to have the jury instructed that the title to the timber was changed by a substantial change of identity. <u>The defendant would only be required to pay the plaintiff the fair value of the timber which he had converted.</u>
    - **Good faith:** If the defendant had appropriated the trees in bad faith, then he would not have been entitled to keep the barrel-hoops.
    - **General rule:** If the defendant had changed something significantly (where "significantly" is defined in one of two ways), and has acted in good faith in taking the raw materials, then he has the right to keep the transformed goods, and <u>pay the person whose raw materials were taken the value of those materials. The definitions are:</u>
        - **1:** <u>Change in the physical identity of the raw materials.</u> E.g., grapes into wine, wheat into bread. Has the identity of the raw materials been changed in character

such that their identity can be said to be destroyed within the meaning of the authorities? **This is the older doctrine.**
- **Rationale:** Difficulty in separating out the original product from the transformed product. Since the original products cannot be identified, it is better to give the property right in them to the person who modified them.
- **2:** Change in the value of the goods: If the transformation provided a big enough change in the market value of the raw materials, then the transformer has the right to the transformed goods.
  - **Rationale:** Allowing the "improver in value" to retain control over the improved goods, and merely pay the market value of the raw materials, means that the improver in value retains the **right to the fruits of his labor.**
    - Allowing the owner of the raw materials to gain title to the improved goods would be, in effect, **allowing that person to reap what he did not sow.**
  - The goal of this is to reward improvers – the doctrine does not allow someone to keep something merely because it has appreciated in value with no effort put into improving it.
- **Reasons for shift from older to newer doctrine:** (1) The equitable nature of the second doctrine, which allows improvers to reap the fruits of their labor; (2) **this test deprivileges the expenditure of physical labor in favor of the expenditure of productive labor.**; (3) The idea of moral desert (reaping what one sows).

NOTE ON EXPLAINING THE PRINCIPLE OF ACCESSION
- Principle of accession can be regarded as an alternative principle of acquisition, distinct from first possession.
  - Like first possession, accession assigns property rights in unowned things, but instead of picking out someone who has expended labor at bringing that thing under his control (as in first possession), the principle of accession assigns the unowned thing to the owner of some prominent other thing,
  - Both first possession and accession identify a singular "winner" in the competition to be the owner of the unowned thing.
  - **Advantage of accession:** It typically identifies this winner w/o her having to do anything, and it **does not encourage the wasteful racing behavior often associated with first possession, discovery, or creation.**
    - Also enhances the incentives to improve property, insofar as new increments in value are automatically assigned to the existing owner of the prominently connected asset.
      - This strength is also a weakness – **accession principle gives rise to unearned windfalls and helps make the rich get richer, as it were.**
- **Arguments for various accession doctrines:** (1) Standard utilitarian arguments; (2) Hume's argument that accession is a function of human psychology (the idea that, from an object related to us, we acquire a relation to all other objects that is related to that first object, and so on).

- o Hume's theory of property generally rests on convention, while the accession principle (like possession) rests on a preference for conforming to a widespread pattern of behavior (e.g. respecting each other's possession) – that could have been otherwise.

THE AD COELUM RULE
- *Edwards v. Sims:* Edwards had discovered a cave under land belonging to him and his wife. Edwards made significant capital improvements to the cave, ultimately turning it into a tourist attraction. A suit was filed against Edwards by another landowner, claiming that a portion of the cave was under his land. The chancellor ordered that a survey be made (involving sending surveyors onto Edwards's land). Edwards sought a writ of prohibition against a judge of the circuit court, to prevent him from enforcing the order.
  - o *Ad Coelum* **right** (as described here): Owner of realty is entitled to the free and unfettered control of his own land above, upon, and beneath the surface. <u>This right can ordinarily not be interfered with or infringed upon by third parties.</u>
  - o **Question:** Whether a court of equity has the right to invade the *ad coelum* right through its agents, for the purpose of ascertaining whether or not Edwards was trespassing upon his neighbor's property.
  - o **Holding:** Writ of prohibition denied.
    - **Rationale:** Followed from the court's determination that there was little differentiation between caves and mines.
      - Per Kentucky law, a court of equity had the inherent power, independent of statute, to compel a mine owner to permit an inspection of the mine at the suit of a party who can show reasonable ground for suspicion that his lands are being trespassed upon.
        - o Court saw no difference in principle between invasion of a mine and invasion of a cave for this purpose.
  - o **Dissent:** Argued (w/o any legal precedent) that the true principle of the *ad coelum* rule should be announced to the effect that a man who owns the surface, without reservation, owns not only the land itself but everything upon, above, or under it which he may subject to his dominion or control.
    - From this, dissent argued that the other landowner suing Edwards had no right to the cave network below his property because he was not exercising dominion and control over it.
    - **Rationale:** One long, extended, <u>reaping without sowing argument</u> – people suing Edwards were trying to leech off of his hard work in turning the cave into a tourist attraction, without having contributed anything to the cave's development.
      - Would have been no profit without Edwards's hard work.

Accretion
- *Nebraska v. Iowa:* Dispute between the states over the boundary line between them, which was defined by the Missouri river. There were marked changes in the course of the river, which led to the boundary disputes.

- **Holding:** Most of the changes had been the result of accretion, and thus the boundary moved with the river's changes (even though the river changed relatively rapidly). <u>However</u>, a boundary change which was the result of a very sudden change was held to be the result of avulsion, and thus the boundary remained where it was fixed before the sudden change.
- **Accretion:** The gradual deposit by water of solid material, producing dry land which was before covered by water.
- **Avulsion:** A sudden change in the course or channel of a body of running water (e.g. river creates an oxbow lake).
    - Avulsion results in no change of boundary lines.
- **Reliction:** This refers to land which was covered by water, but which has been revealed by the imperceptible recession of the water.
- **Erosion:** The gradual and imperceptible wearing away of land (bordering on water) by the natural action of the elements.
- <u>Owners of riparian land that is augmented through the operation of accretion or reliction automatically gain title to the new land. Owners of riparian land which is diminished due to erosion automatically lose title to the lost land.</u>
- These rules are universally followed.
- <u>These rules only come into operation when the boundary is defined as a body of water.</u>

E: BY FIND

- *Armory v. Delamirie* **(England)**: The finder of a lost object has a property right in the object that is ***good against all but the rightful owner of the object.***
    - A finder differs from a true first possessor in two respects: (1) when a finder takes possession of an object, the finder does not thereby become the owner. The object is understood to belong to someone else, the true owner, who cannot be identified or located. (2) The finder has certain duties to the true owner – he is under a legal duty not to convert the object to the finder's own use, or not to deliver the object to anyone other than the true owner.
        - In practice, since the true owner is the only one who could enforce these duties, as time goes by the finder may be able to treat the lost object as if it were not different from the finder's own property.
        - **Rationale - Finder v. Thief:** We want to discourage the theft or conversion of property, so we will naturally award the Finder the original property. We also do not want to have to force Finder 1 to take costly precautions to protect his property.
- *Clark v. Maloney:* Plaintiff finds logs in the bay, ties them up, defendant claims that he found them adrift.
    - **Holding:** Finder 1 versus Finder 2; the court extrapolated from the principle laid down in *Armory* to rule in favor of Finder 1.
    - **Rationale – Finder v. Finder:** We have a strong incentive to settle who owns a chattel. There are efficiency reasons for giving it to Finder 1 (versus Finder 2):

- - - (1) It avoids the problem of forcing Finder 1 to take costly precautions to protect his property.
    - (2) This also promotes the best use of property, and encourages finders to be good stewards of the property in question.
    - (3) Makes it easier for the true owner to regain the property.
- *Anderson v. Gouldberg:* Plaintiff found logs, gained possession by trespass; defendant claimed possession of them preventing plaintiff's possession. Defendant did not own the land on which plaintiff trespassed.
  - Holding: Converter 1 v. Converter 2; Court ruled in favor of Converter 1.
  - Rationale - Thief v. Thief:
    - (1) Again, we want to discourage theft (or a chain of theft), as this is societally inefficient.
    - (2) Furthermore, we don't want to encourage people to assert the rights of third parties. If Thief 2 is able to introduce evidence that property belongs to Owner A, then this would create an administrative nightmare.
    - (3) Makes it easier for the true owner to regain property.
  - There are very few cases between a Converter 1 and a Converter 2. The only other one that we know of, *Russell v. Hill*, reached the opposite decision from this one – it allowed Converter 2 to defeat an action brought by Converter 1 by showing that the true owner of the converted property was Party C.
- These cases are often cited for the proposition that **an action to protect possession of property cannot be defeated by setting up a superior title in a third party (the *jus tertii*).** Defendants cannot invoke *jus tertii* to defeat an action to protect possession.
- Hypothetical situations:
  - Original owner v. Finder: Original owner wins.
  - Finder 1 v. Finder 2: Finder 1 wins.
  - Finder v. Converter: Finder wins.
  - Original owner v. converter: Original owner wins.
  - Thief 1 v. Thief 2: Thief 1 wins.
  - Thief v. Subsequent finder: The thief would arguably win (since the *jus tertii* cannot be invoked).
  - **Transferee v. Finder:** It is most likely that the transferee would win, even if the transferee never had possession of the property. This is because part of the property right is the right to gift or to contract away one's property. If we didn't protect the rights of the transferee, we could not have a functional market economy.
- **A justification** inherent in all of these is that we want to protect the right of the true owner when the true owner has no proof of original ownership. Allowing property to be passed through a chain of finders would make it much more difficult for the original owner to find his property.

F: COMPETING PRINCIPLES OF ORIGINAL ACQUISITION
- All of the following cases involve a conflict between principles of first possession and accession.

- *Fisher v. Steward*: Plaintiff found a swarm of bees in a tree on the defendant's land, marked the tree, and notified the defendant, who cut down the tree and converted the honey to his own use. The court ruled in favor of the defendant.
    - Plaintiff did not have any property in the land or the tree, and did not have any property in the bees.
    - The marking of the tree was a trespass.
    - **Principle:** Captured wild animals belong to the owner of the land where they are captured. This is the principle of *ratione soli*. **Ratione soli is an instance of the principle of accession, while the plaintiffs claimed the bees under a first possession theory.**
    - In disputes between landowners and first possessors, the landowners have generally won.
- *Goddard v. Winchell:* A meteorite fell on land owned by the plaintiff, and embedded itself in the ground there. The grass rights to this land had been leased to a third party (the "tenant"), who permitted another person to dig it out and claim it as his. That person sold the meteorite to the defendant. The title in the meteorite was awarded to the plaintiff. In a subsequent action for damages, the defendant was allowed to keep the meteorite for scientific use, but had to pay the plaintiff damages.
    - The plaintiff's claim to the meteorite was derived from accession (accession because it had fallen on his land and embedded itself into the land). The defendant's claim was derived from first possession (he had been sold the meteorite by its founder).
    - The aerolite was not "unclaimed by any owner," and, because unclaimed, was not abandoned by the lase proprietor.
    - There was no issue of trespass here – the plaintiff's tenant had allowed the other person onto his land to dig out the aerolite.
- *Hannah v. Peel:* Plaintiff, an Army NCO, found a very old brooch on a windowsill in a house which had been recently purchased by the defendant (the house had been requisitioned by the army during WWII). The court ultimately found in favor of the plaintiff, on the ground that the brooch was "lost", was "found" by the plaintiff, and the true owner of the brooch had never been found.
    - Competing theories of first possession (Corporal Hannah) and accession (Peel).
    - The court considered four cases when making its decision:
        - *Armory v. Delamirie* – the finder of an object has a property right in the object which is **good against all but the rightful owner of the object.**
        - *Bridges v. Hawksworth:* The place where a lost article is found does not constitute any exception to the general rule of law, that the finder is entitled to it as against all persons except the owner.
        - *South Staffordshire Water Co. v. Sharman:* The finder (the defendant) in this case was cleaning out a pool on the orders of the plaintiff company, when he found two rings. The court ruled in favor of the plaintiff on the basis (in part) that the possession of land carried with it the possession of everything which was attached to or under that land.
        - *Elwes v. Brigg Gas Co.*: Lessees (the gas co.) found a prehistoric boat when digging to make a gasholder. IT was held that the boat, whether regarded as a mineral or

a part of the soil in which it was embedded, or as a chattel, did not pass to the lessees by the demise, but was the property of the lessor even though the lessor was ignorant of its existence at the time of granting the lease.
- General Rules:
  - (1): The first finder of a thing has a good title to it against all but the true owner, even though the thing is not found on the property of another person. However, this principle is subject to many important exceptions.
    - (a): When the owner of the property is already in possession not merely of the property but also of the thing itself, as in certain circumstances he may undoubtedly be.
    - (b): If anyone finds something as the servant or agent of another, he finds it for his employer.
    - (c): If the finder got possession only through a trespass or other act of wrongdoing, then he obtains no title to the object.
      - Any other result would incentivize trespassing.
- **Case-specific issues:** The court gave less weight to the defendant's interest as owner of the house, on the ground that he had never entered into actual possession of the house before the brooch was found. This seemed to tilt the court away from accession (**Peel**) to first possession (**Hannah**).
- If the brooch had been buried under ground, then per the rule of treasure trove it would belong to the Crown. The doctrine of treasure trove has generally been rejected in American courts (some exceptions include shipwrecks, see above).
- **Mislaid v. Lost Property:** In some American courts, there is a distinction between lost and mislaid property. An object is <u>mislaid</u> when the owner intentionally places it somewhere and then forgets it. An object is <u>lost</u> when the owner is unaware of losing possession of it. Courts that observe the distinction **<u>generally award lost property to the finder, and mislaid property to the owner of the land where it is found.</u>**

G: Adverse Possession

- *Marengo Cave Co. v. Ross:* Lays out the rules for adverse possession:
  - **Possession must be <u>adverse</u>:** This is satisfied if the disseisor does not have permission to use the land.
  - **Possession must be <u>actual</u>:** The disseisor must actually be in possession of the land, and use the land as a property owner would. This is a fact-based judgment, which focuses on concrete things which the disseisor did to possess and change the state of the land; e.g. clearing, mowing, pulling up stumps.
  - **Possession must be <u>exclusive</u>:** The disseisor must be excluding the true owner of the land from the land.
  - **Possession must be <u>open and notorious</u>:** The invasion of the land must be so visible that the owner could readily see that another person was asserting a claim, and must be of such a character as to give notice of invasion to a reasonable person (if actual owner has knowledge, this requirement is met).
  - **Possession must be <u>continuous</u>:** The disseisor must have been continuously occupying the land for the entire period of the statute of limitations (e.g., in NY, for 10 years).

- o Possession must be under <u>adverse under a claim of right</u>: Was the claim adverse under claim of right? There are three approaches to this:
  - **1. Good faith requirement (minority rule):** If the state has this requirement, then the disseisor must subjectively, but mistakenly, believe that he is legally entitled to possession of the property, <u>i.e. that the AP is acting in good faith.</u>
    - **Arg. For:** Moral concerns (no reaping w/o sowing); disincentivizes people from trying to take other peoples' land (AP is a forced, nonconsensual transfer of land with no compensation to original owner).
    - **Arg against:** Evidentiary issues (how to prove good faith?); lower court admin. costs if no need to prove good faith; if goal is to make sure land is stewarded properly then AP in bad faith should be tolerated bec. it is the societally optimal outcome w.r.t. stewardship; disseisor might have a reliance interest in the use of the land.
  - **2. Bad faith requirement (Maine rule):** If the state has this requirement, then the disseisor subjectively believes that he is not legally entitled to possession of the property, <u>i.e. the AP is acting in bad faith.</u> This rule is sometimes called the Maine Rule.
    - **Rationale:** If disseisor enters land knowing it is not theirs, then hypothetically that person must place a very high premium on the land (since they risk suit for trespass).
  - **3. State of mind is irrelevant:** If the state has this requirement, then **all that matters is that the disseisor has not been given permission by the true owner to use the property.**
    - **Arguments:** See above in "Arg. Against" section under Good Faith; personhood justification – over time the disseisor develops a greater attachment to the property, while that of the OP diminishes.
  - **[ONLY IN A FEW STATES] – Color of Title:** A person enters under color of title when he has some legal document, e.g. a deed, will, or judicial decree, that purports to convey title but does not in fact do so because of some legal defect (e.g., grantor did not own the land, or instrument was improperly executed). Only a few states require color of title as an element of AP.
- *Carpenter v. Ruperto:* This case illustrates the principle of a good faith requirement as a condition of obtaining title by adverse possession. Most commentators (both English and American) favor the objective non-permission interpretation of adverse under a claim of right (where state of mind is irrelevant).
- *Howard v. Kunto.* Two important rules:
  - o <u>Establishing requisite possession requires such possession and dominion "as ordinarily marks the conduct of owners in general in holding, managing, and caring for property of like nature and condition."</u>
    - Summer occupancy did not destroy continuity of possession in this case.
      - Continuous as in context of how surrounding land is used. Here the area was used for summer houses.

- An occupant of real property may "**tack**" the adverse use of its predecessors if there is some "reasonable connection" between them (e.g. purchase, devising, inheritance). Whether or not a party can tack also depends on the state of mind requirement in the state.
- **Adverse possession against the government:** Adverse possession claims generally cannot be brought against the government (definitely not the federal government). This is pursuant to the maxim *nullum tempus occurrit regi* – "No time runs against the King."
- *RATIONALES FOR ADVERSE POSSESSION:*
  - (1): Generally, the Adverse Possessor (AP) has a **reliance interest** in the continued property. Recognizing adverse possession means that we are recognizing the reliance interest.
    - **Counter:** The property owner has a stake in the value of the entire property, and allowing someone to adversely possess against that interest will reduce their economic interest.
  - (2): **This disincentivizes allowing landowners to sleep on their rights**. Allowing the owners of property to sleep on their rights for a long time before suing in ejectment (or whatever is appropriate for the occasion) creates an additional administrative burden on the court.
    - **Counter:** Incentivizes AP by bad faith, which incentivizes acting in bad faith. Generally, bad faith is disincentivized by the law.
  - **(3) – AP as a means of "firing a bad steward"**: The landowner who is allowing his property to be lost to an AP claim is a "bad steward" of the land by not making good use of it. Allowing the adverse possessor to gain title to the land serves as a means of rewarding the more efficient user of the land (this goes back to **rewarding the fruits of one's labor**), and thus produces the societally optimal outcome (certainly moreso than allowing a landowner to sleep on his rights).
    - **Counter:** Increases the cost of the land ownership because it requires landowners to monitor their property, which can be expensive.

III: Values Subject to Ownership (Or Not)

A: PROPERTY AND PERSONHOOD
- *Moore v. Regents:* Court ruled that Moore could sue the doctors who took his cells for research purposes for failure to provide informed consent (med. mal), but not for conversion.
  - Court framed the question as "does Moore have a property interest in the cells which were removed from his body?" **and concluded that Moore did not have a property right in his cells.**
    - Common law principles of **accession and abandonment were not applied** – under accession theory, Moore is still entitled to damages for the market value of his input (the cells), and he did not intend to give up his cells for the purpose which they were used.

- Rationales for decision:
  - <u>Desire to defer creation of a property right in cells to the legislature</u> (no belief in judicial lawmaking).
    - (1) <u>Policy</u> – extending a property right to these cells would open up any scientists who used the Moore cell line to liability for conversion. This would have a chilling effect on medical research (extension of strict liability reduces activity levels).
    - (2) <u>Societal benefit</u> – society benefits from the improvements in medical care which research on the Moore cell line brings about. We might see the free provision of those inputs as being compensated by advances in medical sciences.
    - (3) <u>Moral issues</u> – we would be undermining human dignity by allowing people to sell their body parts (creation of property interest in body → property in body is alienable).
      - Lockean **reaping without sowing** is also a concern (Why should Moore own a right in the cell line when others did all the work?)
  - <u>Majority and dissenters treated property as a "bundle of sticks".</u>
- *Kremen v. Cohen:* Judge Kozinski allowed Kremen to sue Network Solutions for the conversion of the website sex.com (**holding that there was a property right in a domain name**).
  - Kozinksi rejected all the policy arguments which the court in *Moore* had used to decline to extend a property right. He believed that greater regulation of domain name registration would be a good idea. Both cases approached the question of whether the plaintiff has a property interest, and took a similar approach to how one determines whether something is property.
    - Increased costs in protecting domain name is desirable; domain names were underprotected in judge's view.
    - **Rationales for different outcome to** *Moore:* (1) <u>Social utility of research:</u> Medical research is more valuable than pornography. (2) Kremen had a well-defined interest and a claim to exclusivity (exclusive authority over the domain name), while Moore did not have as strong a claim.

Demsetz: *Toward a Theory of Property Rights*

- Theorizes that <u>a primary function of property rights is that of guiding incentives to achieve a greater internalization of externalities.</u> Every cost and benefit associated with social interdependencies is a potential externality.
- <u>The cost of a transaction in the rights between the parties (internalization) must exceed the gains from internalization.</u>
- **Theory:** Property rights develop to internalize externalities when the gains of internalization become larger than the cost of internalization. Increased internalization, in the main, results from changes in economic values, changes which stem from the development of new technology and the opening of new markets, changes to which old property rights are poorly attuned.

- **Empirical analysis:** The development of property rights among American aboriginals. Demsetz, building on anthropological analyses by Leacock and Speck, argued that as the beaver trade became more and more valuable, American Indians internalized the costs of overhunting of beavers (a kind of tragedy of the commons) by developing property rights associated with the beaver (for example the division of hunters into several somewhat organized bands in order to hunt more efficiently, the appropriation of pieces of land for each group to hunt exclusively, and the marking of beaver houses.
- **Inverse Demsetz:** If, in an established property right, the cost of internalization becomes higher than the benefits of internalization (whether because the costs increase and the benefits remain stable, or because the benefits decrease), then we would theoretically see a weakening of property rights in favor of more "common" rights.
- **Notes:** This theory is built around the costs and benefits of property rights. One such cost is the cost of excluding others – marking boundary lines, putting up fences, suing trespassers, etc.
    - If an asset becomes less valuable, will less effort be expended on protecting property rights in the asset, in extreme situations resulting in abandonment of the asset into the public domain?

Radin: *Property and Personhood*

- Some things are so closely related to personhood that they should not be considered property (e.g. wedding rings)
- Can gauge the strength or significance of someone's relationship with an object by the kind of pain that would be occasioned by its loss.
    - **Object is closely related to one's personhood if its loss causes pain that cannot be relieved by the object's replacement.**
    - Opposite of holding an object that has become a part of oneself is holding an object that is perfectly replaceable with other goods of equal market value. **One holds such an object for purely instrumental reasons.**
        - Archetype of this is money.
- Once we admit that a person can be bound up with an external "thing" in some constitutive sense, we can argue that, by virtue of this connection the person should be accorded broad liberty with respect to control over that "thing"
    - **There is such a thing as property for personhood because people become bound up with "things".**
- **Property in one's body:** If it makes sense to say that one owns one's body, then on the embodiment theory of personhood, the body is quintessentially personal property because it is literally constitutive of one's personhood.
    - Idea of property in one's body means that body parts can become fungible commodities (e.g. one can sell blood).
    - Though the general idea of property for personhood means that the boundary between person and thing cannot be a bright line, the idea of property seems to require some perceptible boundary.

B: PUBLIC RIGHTS – WATERWAYS AND AIRWAYS

- Navigable Waters
  - Navigable water is treated as an inherently public resource.
    - **Definition:** In English law, navigable waters were defined to mean those waters subject to the ebb and flow of the tides (therefore, submerged land under rivers and lakes not subject to the tides was subject to private ownership).
      - King as sovereign owned and controlled all navigable waters within the realm, and presumptively owned the land beneath navigable waters.
      - Absent a grant to the contrary, owner of land bordering on a non-navigable body of water owned the submerged land to the thread of the current, or center line of the river, or the lake on which the land abutted.
    - Private owners of waters that were nontidal but navigable in fact could not interfere with public navigation, provided that those wishing to traverse such waters could obtain access without trespassing.
  - **United States:** All bodies of water that are navigable in fact (including non-tidal waters, e.g. Great Lakes, Lake Champlain) are navigable waters, and are thus treated as an inherently public resource.
  - Traditional reasons why state holds title to submerged lands beneath navigable waterways:
    - Navigation
    - Fishing
    - Commerce
- Navigable Airspace
  - *United States v. Causby*: When flights are made within the navigable airspace, without any physical invasion of the property of the landowners over which the flights are made, then there has been no taking of property.
    - *Ad coelum* rule does not apply above a certain height above land.
    - Air is a public highway.
    - **Rationale:** Recognizing private claims to the airspace would lead to tragedy of the anticommons (too many rightsholders), and would seriously interfere with the control and development of air travel.
  - Airspace, other than that immediately above the land, is part of the public domain.
  - After *Causby*, navigable airspace in the USA has assumed roughly same status as navigable waterways.

THE PUBLIC TRUST DOCTRINE
- *Illinois Central R.R. Co. v. Illinois* (U.S. 1892): Plaintiff railroad held title to submerged lands under Chicago lakefront. Suit was to obtain a judicial determination of the title of those lands.
  - **Background:** State had granted title to the submerged land per an act of the Illinois legislature.
  - **Holding:**

- **(1)** State held the rights to submerged land under navigable but nontidal water (Lake Michigan) same as it did submerged land under tide water.
- **(2)** Title is different in character from that which the United States holds in public lands open to pre-emption and sale – <u>it is a title held in trust for the people of the state for navigation, fishing, and commerce ("Public Trust Doctrine").</u>
  - State cannot abdicate its trust over property, <u>even with an act of the Legislature</u> in which the whole people have an interest.
- **(3)** State may grant parcels of land to private bodies so long as:
  - **(3)(a)** <u>The grants are to benefit public navigation, fishing, or commerce,</u> OR
  - **(3)(b)** <u>The parcels can be disposed of without detriment to the public interest in the lands and waters remaining</u>.
- The grant of the land to the railroad by the Illinois Legislature was necessarily revocable.
- **Rationale:** Granting whole of submerged lands to the railroad allowed the railroad to exert monopoly control over the waterfront, with subsequent detrimental effects on rent and commercial development.
- **Dissent:** Illinois can take the rights and property of the railroad company in the land by a constitutional condemnation of them (a <u>"legislative taking"</u>).
- **Note 4:** Per later SCOTUS rulings, the public trust doctrine is grounded in state law. This means that the states are free to repudiate the trust, either by statute or by an amendment to their state constitutions.

TRANSFORMATION OF THE PUBLIC TRUST DOCTRINE
- Doctrine led a quiet life until 1970, when Prof. Joseph Sax argued that the doctrine could be employed as an effective tool for environmental protection.
- Public trust doctrine effectively transformed from a doctrine about public access to commercial navigation into a doctrine about preservation of natural resources.
  - **(1)** Raises the question of whether the underlying purpose of the doctrine – that title to certain resources must remain in government hands – is necessarily well-designed to meet preservationist ends.
    - Illinois courts, for example, have been much more willing to go along with development projects where title remains in government hands.
      - Cumulatively, Illinois decisions do not suggest that a doctrine focused on legal title will consistently function to preserve natural resources from development.
  - **(2)** Raises another question of whether this is consistent with <u>principles of democratic control over state-owned resources.</u>
    - In some more recent decisions, the public trust doctrine has been used to invalidate projects <u>in which all relevant, publicly accountable, governmental bodies have signed off, deeming the project to be in the public interest.</u>

- - o **(3)** Concerns the scope of the doctrine. Most decisions enforcing the doctrine involve resources that have some connection with navigable water.
      - Furthermore, land owned by the United States federal government is not subject to the public trust doctrine – it is freely alienable by the government.
  - **Note on purprestures:** Closely related to the public trust doctrine is the problem of encroachments by private persons on navigable waterways or public highways.
    - o These sorts of encroachments are called **purprestures.**
      - At common-law, purprestures were controlled by public nuisance actions, **not** by trespass law.
  - *State of Oregon ex rel. Thornton v. Hay* **(OR 1969):** Resort owners wanted to build fences to keep public out of dry sand areas (land between mean high tide line and vegetation), which they owned. Issue was whether the state had the power to limit the record owner's (deed holder's) use and enjoyment of the dry-sand area.
    - o **Holding:** The state has the power to prevent the resort owners from keeping the public out of the dry sand areas.
      - Neither the state (owners of the wet sand area) nor the resort owners (owners of the dry sand area) **had the full bundle of rights normally connoted by the term "estate in fee simple."**
      - **Rationale:** Court relied on **custom** – public had enjoyed dry-sand area as a recreational adjunct of the wet-sand area **since the beginning of the state's political history.**
      - Requirements to claim something by custom (from Blackstone):
        - **(1)** Custom must be ancient – it must have been used for so long that **"the memory of man runneth not to the contrary"**
        - **(2)** The right must be exercised without interruption. The right does **not** need to be exercised continuously, but there must be no interruptions by **anyone possession a paramount right.**
        - **(3)** Customary use must be peaceable and free from dispute.
        - **(4)** Customary use must be reasonable (satisfied by evidence that the public always made use of the land in a manner appropriate to the land and to the usages of the community)
        - **(5)** Custom must be certain (satisfied here by visible boundaries of the dry-sand area and by the character of the land)
        - **(6)** Custom must be obligatory – in this case, meaning that it must not be left to the option of each landowner whether or not he will recognize the public's right to go upon the dry-sand area for recreational purposes.
        - **(7)** Custom must not be repugnant or inconsistent with other customs, or with other law.
      - Court did not rely on easements because prescriptive easements apply only to the specific tract of land before the court – **would create huge administrative mess**, since court would be filled for years with tract-by-tract easement litigation.
        - Also, problem with consent – cannot get a prescriptive easement if one has consent.

- Furthermore, custom appropriate because of unique nature of the lands in question.
    - **Problems with custom:** Can impede resource preservation, undermines property rights of landlords, can result in inefficient land uses, <u>disincentivizes upkeep of beach area</u>, can incite rushing behavior and the tragedy of the commons.
  - **Note 4:** A number of states have used the public trust doctrine to hold that all or part of the dry sand beach is inherently public property.
    - Florida, Texas, and Hawaii have joined Oregon in using versions of the customary rights doctrine to declare public rights of access to dry sand beaches.
    - Other states have rejected entreaties to declare beaches public property on any theory.
  - **Note 5:** Overall trend seems to be toward greater public rights or open access to beaches.
  - **Note 6:** Public trust doctrine may or may not be subject to legislative revision. In some states (e.g. Illinois) public trust doctrine is viewed as a fixed qualification on title and so cannot be revised by the legislature.
    - Doctrine of public prescription is probably subject to legislative revision, although since prescriptive easements are property rights, the government might have to condemn these rights and pay just compensation in order to eliminate them.
    - Doctrine of customary rights is <u>**clearly subject to legislative revision.**</u>
- Carol Rose – *The Comedy of the Commons.*
  - New version of "inherent publicness" argument has appeared in a series of cases expanding public access to waterfront property (especially dry sand area) for the purposes of recreation.
    - New beach cases usually employ one of three theoretical bases:
      - <u>(1)</u> Public trust theory – private rights subordinate to public's trust rights.
      - <u>(2)</u> Prescriptive or dedicatory theory – period of public usage gives rise to an implied grant or gift from private owners.
      - <u>(3)</u> Theory of "custom".
    - **Arguments in favor of private ownership:** Uncertainty about property rights invites conflicts and squanders resources. Public access turns waterfront into a commons where no one any incentive to purchase the property, care for it, or invest in it.
    - **Arguments in favor of public ownership:**
      - <u>(1)</u> Beaches and waterways are "plenteous" and "boundless", and thus it is not worth the effort to create a system of resource management for them.
        - Per Demsetz, this is not necessarily true.
      - <u>(2)</u> Governmental body might be the most useful manager where many persons desire access or control over a given property, but they are too numerous and their individual stakes too small to express their preferences in market transactions (anticommons).

- o **Rose's argument:** Movement towards making beaches an open access resource can be explained and justified on the ground that this permits social contact among a large number of persons of mixed backgrounds.

IV: Owner Sovereignty and Its Limits
A: Criminal and Civil Trespass Actions
- *State v. Shack:* The complainant employed migrant workers for his seasonal needs, and housed them on his land. Defendants entered onto his property to aid these workers (one defendant was there to offer medical services, and the other was there to discuss a legal issue with a migrant worker), and were arrested for trespass.
    - o The court performed a <u>"balancing test"</u> between the right of the landowner to exclude the aid workers and the rights of the migrant workers to receive services and aid.
    - o <u>We might actually be seeing the court trying to redistribute some property rights to the workers – i.e. the conflict is arising from socioeconomic concerns.</u>
    - o This case is interesting because it makes us think that trespass is not a bright-line rule. There are two ways to read this case:
        - One is that this carves out an exception to the trespass statutes to allow people aiding migrant workers to enter private land to benefit those workers.
        - Another way to read this is that the NJ Supreme Court is subjecting the rights of private landowners to a balancing test (which is why this case alarms some commentators).
- *Intel v. Hamidi*: Hamidi worked for Intel and was dissatisfied with his treatment. After his employment ended, he was sending emails to Intel's employees using mailing lists that he acquired. The emails contained messages that were upsetting to Intel, so they sued for trespass to chattel.
    - o **Question:** Can Intel sue for trespass to chattel for Hamidi sending the email to Intel's employees?
    - o **Holding:** No. There is no property right in the internet for sending email, except in the case of spam.
        - Because there is no evidence of interference with the function of Intel's servers/network, there cannot be trespass to chattel.
            - Employee time, which was interfered with, is not considered a chattel.
    - This is not a boundary crossing claim, so analogizing to trespass to land didn't work.
    - **Epstein's theory:** Argued that a rule of computer server inviolability (extending real property rules of trespass to computer servers) would create efficient outcomes.
    - **Lessig's theory:** Argued that parcelization would require some kind of individually negotiated license between the proprietor of the computer network and each visitor, and that these negotiations would possibly create a cyber-anticommons.
    - **Problems:** Epstein's theory leads to trouble with licensing and permission (too many holdouts, high administration costs in getting permission from people).

- o **Counter**: since actual damages are necessary, does that incentivize companies to stop upgrading so that any potential intrusions will causes damages and thus they'll be able to maintain an action?
- **Dissent**: The two dissenting opinions agree with Epstein's theories.
- **Note 1**: According to the majority in *Hamidi*, no legal remedy other than self-help for an intentional trespass to personal property that does no injury to the property.
- **Note 2**: Another way to view *Hamidi* is that it simply limits the available remedies for trespass to chattels to damages.
- **Note 6**: Most far-reaching decision in *Hamidi* was whether cyberspace should be subject to parcelization.

B: Self-Help

- Property owners are entitled to take a variety of steps to protect or enforce their property rights w/o the direct involvement of the legal system. These measures are what is known as **self help.**
- **Distinction between rights and privileges** from W. N. Hohfeld: **A right** is a claim that one person has against one or more others, which corresponds to a duty that these others have towards the one with the right. **A privilege** is a freedom to act in certain ways w/o interference from others, which corresponds to a "no-right" in the others to interfere with the one exercising the privilege. **A privilege permits but does not compel a person to do certain things.**
  - o **Self-help can be thought of as a type of privilege associated with ownership.**
- *Berg v. Wiley:* Defendant landlord exercised self-help to try and evict plaintiff tenant from premises which he owned. **The court ruled that a landlord could not use self-help at all, even peaceable self-help, to try and evict a tenant. Landlords looking to displace tenants had to use the judicial process.**
  - o Defendant's lockout of plaintiff could not be excused on the ground that Berg abandoned or surrendered the leasehold.
  - o **Common law rule:** The common law rule is that a landlord can rightfully use self-help to retake leased premises from a tenant in possession without incurring liability for wrongful eviction **provided that two conditions are met:**
    - 1. The landlord is legally entitled to possession, such as where a tenant holds over the lease term or where a tenant breaches a lease containing a reentry clause.
    - 2. The landlord's means of reentry are peaceable.
  - o **Rationale for holding:** It was long the policy of the law to discourage landlords from taking the law into their own hands, and use self-help to dispossess tenants in circumstances which were likely to result in breaches of the peace were discouraged.
    - Legislature's purpose in enacting a forcible entry and unlawful detainer statute was to prevent people claiming a right of entry or possession of lands from redressing their own wrongs by entering into possession in a violent and forcible manner.

- o Other courts have held that self-help in the context of commercial landlord-tenant disputes is still permitted.
- o In jurisdictions which still permit self-help, <u>recovery of possession must still be accomplished without a breach of the peace.</u>
- *Williams v. Ford Motor Credit Co.*: Court upheld the seizure of personal property via self-help methods, since the seizure did not constitute a breach of the peace.
  - o <u>Self-help methods can be used to repossess or dispose of personal property, provided that in doing so there is no breach of the peace.</u>
  - o Most courts have concluded that procedural due process does not apply to self-help repossessions because such a repossession does not entail state action.
  - o Replevin and garnishment proceedings require due process (thus giving owners of personal property significantly protection that they get in a self-help repossession).
- Policy reasons for difference in treatment between real property and personal property:

C: EXCEPTIONS TO THE RIGHT TO EXCLUDE

1. Necessity

- *Ploof v. Putnam:* An exception to the right of property owners to exclude others is ***necessity.*** Necessity allows for people to enter onto another's land, and interfere with their personal property, in order to preserve human life or chattels. **A person entering onto another's property for reasons of necessity cannot be found guilty of trespass.**
  - o Necessity is an **incomplete privilege.** The person entering onto another's property for purposes of necessity is liable for any damages incurred to the property which he is using. ***E.g. Viincent v. Lake Erie Transp. Co.***

2. Custom

- *McConico v. Singleton:* The court ruled that the defendant was not guilty of trespassing onto the plaintiff's unenclosed, unimproved lands because there was a custom of allowing hunters to enter rural unenclosed land in pursuit of game without first obtaining permission of the owner.
  - o Laws which permit anyone to hunt on rural land unless "No Hunting" or "No Trespassing" signs have been prominently posted remain on the books in many states. These laws impose an affirmative burden of notification on the possessor of land in order to assert the right to exclude. If the owner does not make the required notification, then the right to exclude is subordinate to the customary right to hunt on unenclosed and uncultivated land owned by another.
  - o The trend appears to be moving away from presumed access for hunters towards a requirement of owner permission to hunt.
  - o Right to roam laws have been adopted in some countries in the 21st Century. This can be seen as an example of inverse-Demsetz (the costs of internalization not outweigh the benefits of internalization).

3. Public Accommodations Laws

- The law distinguishes between property not open to the public (e.g. homes and factories) and property that offers itself as a "public accommodation." Owners of property not open to the public have long enjoyed broad, sovereign authority to exclude others. However, owners

of public accommodations (e.g. hotels, restaurants) have a much more qualified right to exclude.
- o **Public businesses are subject to a general duty of nondiscrimination among customers, meaning they must provide services to customers on a first-come, first-served basis, and they must charge customers only reasonable rates for the services they provide.**
    - These implied duties are nowadays focused on a narrow list of businesses associated with travel, generally referred to as "inn keepers and common carriers."
        - There has been significant debate over the reasons which led to this narrowing.
            - o **(1)** One argument is that this narrowing applied only to those occupations that continued to exhibit effective monopoly.
            - o **(2)** Another argument is that common carrier duties were imposed on businesses that exhibited a number of indicators that the enterprise was considered "public."
            - o **(3)** A third argument is that the narrowing of public accommodations duties to innkeepers and common carriers was a product of the Jim Crow era of segregation.
    - **Two important duties:**
        - (1) The duty to serve any person who requested service, provided that it was available.
        - (2) The duty to charge prices that were "reasonable." This did not meant that they had to charge exactly the same price to different recipients of the same service.
- o The category of enterprises known as innkeepers and common carriers eventually came to be known as public accommodations. Modern public accommodations laws have been influenced by anti-discrimination laws, most prominently Title II of the Civil Rights Act of 1964.

4. Public Policy

- The most general exception to the right to exclude (which has been fleshed out the most by courts in NJ, of all places) is that owner sovereignty should give way to considerations of public policy. **In this conception, the right to exclude is always subject to a balancing test in which competing social interests must be weighed.**
- *State v. Shack:* The complainant employed migrant workers for his seasonal needs, and housed them on his land. Defendants entered onto his property to aid these workers (one defendant was there to offer medical services, and the other was there to discuss a legal issue with a migrant worker), and were arrested for trespass.
    - o The court performed a **"balancing test"** between the right of the landowner to exclude the aid workers and the rights of the migrant workers to receive services and aid.
    - o **We might actually be seeing the court trying to redistribute some property rights to the workers – i.e. the conflict is arising from socioeconomic concerns.**

- o This case is interesting because it makes us think that trespass is not a bright-line rule. There are two ways to read this case:
  - One is that this carves out an exception to the trespass statutes to allow people aiding migrant workers to enter private land to benefit those workers.
  - Another way to read this is that the NJ Supreme Court is subjecting the rights of private landowners to a balancing test (which is why this case alarms some commentators).
- *Uston v. Resorts International Hotel, Inc.*: Uston, a professional blackjack card-counter, was excluded from a casino operated by the defendant. The NJ Supreme Court ruled that the casino could not exercise a right to exclude Uston from the premises.
  - o This was in part a conflict between the common-law right to exclude, and statutory regimes which have overruled parts of the common law (in this case, the Casino Control Commission).
  - o **Rationales:** The court laid down two rationales for its ruling in favor of Uston.
    - (1): The Commission alone had the authority to exclude patrons based upon their strategies for playing licensed casino games, and thus any common-law right to exclude was abrogated by the act establishing the Commission.
    - (2): The court rejected the idea that Resorts International Hotel had a common-law right to exclude anyone at all for any reason. The basis for this ruling was that **property owners did not have a legitimate interest in unreasonably excluding particular members of the public when they open their premises for public use.**
      - The court noted the current majority American rule disregarded the right of reasonable access, and granted to proprietors of amusement places an absolute right to arbitrarily eject or exclude any person consistent with state and federal civil rights law.
        - o The NJ Supreme Court had rejected this standard, in favor of the idea that "the more private property is devoted to public use, the more it must accommodate the rights which inhere in individual members of the general public who use that property."
  - o In sum, the court ruled that, absent a valid Commission regulation excluding card-counters, Uston was free to use his card-counting strategy at the tables.

5. Antidiscrimination Laws
- *Shelley v. Kraemer:* Appellants, a black family, bought a house from a white seller in a neighborhood. The house was under a restrictive covenant restricting ownership to whites. Respondents were white neighbors who sought to block the sale of the property on the basis of the restrictive covenant.
  - o **Covenants:** A covenant is a private agreement between landowners to restrict and regulate private land use. Restrictive covenants in this context are those which discriminated based on race (the covenant sought to regulate the user of the property rather than the use).
    - **Covenants run with the land – they are binding on all people that buy the property which is subject to the covenants.** Courts began to enforce

covenants (racial or otherwise) starting in the 1920s. Racial covenants were encouraged before WWII by banks and mortgage lenders, as well as by the government through one of its agencies.
- o **Holding:** The Court held that enforcement of the covenant by the government (which the Missouri Supreme Court had upheld) was a violation of the Equal Protection Clause. Once the Kraemers went to court and tried to enforce the covenant, this constituted **state action**, which in this instance was not permitted per the Equal Protection Clause.
    - Of note is that the Court did not ban racial covenants per se – merely their enforcement using the state apparatus (including the courts). **A mere voluntary agreement among neighbors not to sell to blacks would not be state action, and hence is a permissible incidence of owner sovereignty.** New covenants continued to be created up until the Fair Housing Act was signed in 1968.
- o It is widely assumed that the owner of a private house has the right to exclude based on race (and, more generally, protected categories). We could develop a line of argument pursuant to *Shelley* that this form of enforcement constitutes a form of state action.

Present Interest	Magic Words (proper names bolded)	Typical Future Interests
Fee Simple Absolute • Largest package of rights in the modern day; presumed to give all that O has unless O indicates otherwise.	[At common law]: "To A and his/her heirs" [Modern]: The above, plus "To A", "To A in FS"	None.
(Defeasible Fee) **Fee Simple Determinable** • Defeasible in favor of grantor. • Ends automatically upon the occurrence of a named event. • Clock for adverse possession (AP) begins ticking the second that the event occurs.	Language of Duration: "As long as", "So long as", "while", "during", and "until"	Possibility of reverter (in the grantor).
(Defeasible Fee) **Fee Simple Subject to Condition Subsequent** • Defeasible in favor of grantor. • Doesn't end automatically; requires action by grantor or successor. • Clock for AP begins ticking once reverters initiate measures to kick the disseisor off the property.	Language of Condition: Usually contains reference to "right of entry"; "but if", "on condition that", "provided that", "provided however", "if"	Right of Entry/Power of Termination (in grantor).
(Defeasible Fee) **Fee Simple Subject to Executory Limitation** • Defeasible in favor of 3rd party grantee. • Conventional wisdom: FSSEL automatically cut short if some event occurs (more like FSD in this regard)	Language: Same sort of language as we would see in either FSD or FSSCS. Example: O grants Blackacre to M, but if Condition X occurs, then to N.	Executory interest in the grantee [in the example, grantee is N]. Cuts short/divests prior interest. **Springing executory interest:** Divests interest in grantor. **Shifting executory interest:** Divests interest in grantee (third party, as in example).
Fee Tail • Now almost completely abolished.	"To A and the heirs of his body" "To A and his issue."	Reversion (in the grantor).

• Attempts to create fee tail in most states lead to creation of fee simple absolute.		
Life Estate • Ends with the death of a named person, usually holder of the estate. • Alienable by gift or sale. If holder sells the life estate, the purchaser has a <u>life estate pur autre vie</u> – a life estate according to A's lifespan. • New owner would lose property to A's devisees or heirs when A dies.	"To A for life." **Vested sub. to complete divestment example:** O grants B to M for life, then to N, but if C occurs, then to K. (N has a vested remainder subject to complete divestment, K has a contingent remainder). **Vested sub. to partial divestment example:** O grants B to A for life, then to A's children. D is the only child alive at the time. D has a vested remainder sub. to partial divestment.	Reversion (in the grantor) Remainder (in grantee): [Possessory upon natural termination of prior estate] • **Indefeasibly Vested:** Identity of the takers is known and there is no other contingency. • **Vested Subject to Complete Divestment:** If the occurrence of a condition can cause the interest to shift to someone else. • **Vested subject to partial divestment:** If the class of takers is not closed. • **Contingent:** Takers unknown or there is a condition to be fulfilled.

FAIR HOUSING ACT
- The FHA prohibits a range of discriminatory behaviors against members of certain specified protected classes in the housing field, with certain exceptions. Over the years, the FHA has been amended to add protected classes, such as the disabled.
    - **Exemptions (important for our purposes):** Three particular exemptions.
        - **1.** Owners of 3 or fewer single family homes, but the exemption only applies to one sale of one such home within any 24-month period, and the owner cannot advertise or use a real estate agent to broker the sale.
        - **2. <u>The Mrs. Murphy exemption:</u>** If a landlord lives in a building with three or fewer other apartments to rent (i.e. landlord and three or fewer other families), then she is exempt from Section 3604 of the FHA.
        - **3. Religious exemptions/club exemptions:** Religious organizations may restrict the sale of housing to persons of the same religion, unless membership in the religion is restricted on account of race, color, or national origin. Furthermore, private clubs may restrict the provision of lodgings to their members.
- Online publishers are not liable for the content of user-generated materials that appear on their websites, per statute.

V: The Forms of Ownership

A: THE ANGLO-AMERICAN SYSTEM OF ESTATES
Notes
- If the holder of a fee simple absolute dies intestate and has no heirs according to the state intestacy statute, then his property escheats to the state.

- There always has to be someone ready to take, and if the grantor has not given everything away, then a supporting reversion is retained.
- When listing the holders of future interests in a question, make sure to mention the quality of the title which the holder of a future interest has (e.g. A has a life estate, B has a vested remainder subject to partial divestment in fee simple absolute).
- If someone has an executory interest, make sure to specify whether it is springing or shifting.
- If conveyance can be construed as being either FSD or FSSCS, the preferred construction is in favor of FSSCS (from *Toscano*).

Flexibility and Numerus Clausus
- Merrill & Smith, *Optimal Standardization in the Law of Property: The Numerus Clausus Principle*
    - Standardize property rules so that the transaction costs are lower.
        - This is especially true for external costs: if A and B set up some special relationship, then any outside parties interested in A's or B's property will have to do additional research to figure out whether the property is burdened by the special relationship.
            - By limiting property rules to a closed set of options, we reduce the transaction costs.

B: MEDIATING CONFLICTS BETWEEN OWNERS: CONFLICT OVER TIME

WASTE: The holder of a life estate will tend to favor current consumption and investments that produce a quick return. In contrast, the holders of remainders are likely to prefer conservation of the asset and longer-term investments.

- *Brokaw v. Fairchild:* Four houses next to one another each held in life estate by one of four children with the other three in remainder to each house. Holder of one wanted to demolish it and build an apartment complex. The other three sued for waste.
    - **Doctrine:** The holder of a life estate has the right to make use of a property, but does not have the power to make fundamental alterations to the property (exercise ownership and dominion). The life estate has to pass to the holders of remainders in the condition in which it was received – **no fundamental changes.**
    - Court does not take into account the motives and purposes of those bringing suit for waste.
    - Court distinguishes *Melms v. Pabst Brewing* on the facts – the house there was the only residence in an industrial area, whereas here the neighborhood was a nice neighborhood.
        - The *Melms* approach provided the life tenant with greater scope to change the characteristic of the property – if there is some sort of drastic change in circumstances to the property, the life tenant has the right to change the property.
            - This approach gives a lot greater flexibility.
- Forms of waste: Affirmative and permissive waste (ameliorative waste is a subset of the former).

- **Affirmative Waste:** A type of misfeasance, which occurs when the life tenant undertakes some affirmative act on the property that is unreasonable and causes "excess" damage to the reversionary or remainder interest.
  - <u>Defined in terms of what is regarded as the "normal" use of the property.</u>
  - Extraction of minerals (e.g. mining or logging) is waste unless that extraction was already occurring on the land at the beginning of the life estate. Rate of extraction must be "normal."
  - <u>The Brokaw case is a case involving affirmative waste.</u>
- **Permissive Waste:** A type of nonfeasance which occurs when the life tenant fails to take some action with regard to the property, and the failure to act is unreasonable and causes excess damage to the remainder or reversion.
  - Again, conceptions of normal behavior serve to define the baseline against which liability is to be determined.
  - **Examples:** Failing to pay taxes, <u>allowing an adverse possessor to remain on the land.</u>
- **Ameliorative waste:** A type of affirmative act by the life tenant that significantly changes the property but results in an increase, rather than a diminution, in its market value.
  - **Traditional view (*Brokaw*):** Ameliorative waste is just another type of affirmative waste, and is not allowed.
  - **Modern view (*Melms*):** Ameliorative waste is permitted if it can be justified by changed circumstances.
  - Today, the *Brokaw* approach is only followed in a minority of jurisdictions. The law of waste has become more flexible – generally, the greater one's interest, the more freedom one gets as owner.

VALUATION OF INTERESTS
- Remember that the cost today is not equivalent to the cost tomorrow.

RESTRAINTS ON ALIENATION
- Generally struck down by courts; direct restraints on alienation are held void as **contrary to public policy.**
- Efforts to use defeasible fees or executory limitations to effectuate complete restraints on alienation are similarly void.
- *Morse v. Blood:* Will granted decedent's wife a fee simple determinable in an estate, the event being that she could not alienate any part of the estate (no matter how small) to any of either his or her relatives.
  - **Holding:** Although a condition against alienation to particular classes of people is generally good, such a condition may be so vexatious as practically to prohibit all alienation for at least a limited time. Therefore, the court struck down the provision as an unallowable restraint on alienation.
  - Court took particular note of the fact that the condition could be triggered by a very small action, possibly even innocently, and the fact that the condition was inconsistent with itself and the terms of the grant (if plaintiff breached, the property would go to her late husband's heirs).

- **Note 2:** Courts will uphold restraints on alienation for a limited period of time if they appear to be reasonably related to some family estate planning objective.
  - However, if restraint on alienation appears to be designed to discourage remarriage (<u>restraint on marriage</u>), then the court will strike it down.
- **Note 3 – Rationale for the policy against restraints on alienation:**
  - <u>(1)</u> Owner autonomy – the power to alienate prevents owners from becoming slaves to their property.
  - <u>(2)</u> Right to transfer has efficiency justifications – <u>free alienabilty permits things to be reallocated from one person to another so as to allow those who place a higher value on the asset to end up in control of it.</u>
    - If transaction costs were zero, this would result in all things ending up in the hands of persons who valued them the most.
  - <u>(3)</u> We can think of free alienation as the primary way in which society changes assignments of responsibility for the management of resources. When one owner/gatekeeper gets tired of performing the role of asset manager, he can transfer managerial responsibility to someone else more eager to take on the role.
    - This method of changing managers taps into local knowledge and probably generates less friction than other methods, such as adverse possession, eminent domain, or having the state decide who gets to be the manager.
- *Mountain Brow Lodge v. Toscano:* If one has a fee simple subject to any of three kinds of restraints, then the restraints are invalid. If, however, **the restraint on alienation is partial, then it might be permissible if it is seen to be reasonable.**
  - Grant included language that could be construed as a restraint on alienation or a FSSCS.
  - If the restraint is so narrow that it creates an effective restraint on alienation, then that restraint will also be struck down.
  - **Holding**: restraint on alienation struck down, but the other language in the grant was interpreted to be a fee simple subject to a condition subsequent.
    - The court interprets it this way so that it doesn't end up disincentivizing donations to charity.

NOTES ON THE RULE AGAINST PERPETUITIES (RAP)
[[Remember not to spend more than a sentence on this in the exam]]
- **Formulation of the RAP:** *"No interest unless it must vest, if at all, not later than 21 years after some life in being at the creation of the interest."*
  - The rule defines a time period (lives in being plus 21 years) and asks them whether within the time period we will know whether or not certain types of questions will be resolved. These questions have to do with uncertainty about vesting in interest, not necessarily vesting in possession.
    - <u>RAP is not a rule against interests lasting too long.</u>
- **Interests subject to the RAP:** Contingent remainders, executory interests, and vested remainders subject to partial divestment (i.e. subject to open). All other future interests, including those retained by the grantor (reversions, rights of entry, possibilities of reverter) and other types of vested remainders are <u>not</u> subject to the RAP.

- The RAP does not prevent "perpetual" or even very long-lasting interests. Instead, **the RAP prohibits the creation of contingent interests that are not certain to vest within a prescribed time period.**
- Rationales for the RAP:
    - (1): **Long-lasting contingencies about title can impair alienation.** Few people will want to buy property with unresolved contingencies about ownership hanging over it.
    - (2): **There are concerns about giving the dead too much control over the ownership and use of resources by the living.** The RAP basically allows testators to keep ownership contingent for one generation into the future plus the next generation up to the traditional age of majority. **The judges who devised the rule thought that these are the only people that a testator can really have any knowledge of or benevolence towards.**
    - (3): **The RAP is sometimes associated with the objective of breaking up large, potentially overly aristocratic estates.**
        - RAP creates a barrier to "dynastic impulses" by making it hard for elite families to create various contingent interests lasting far into the future.
- **Reforms:** Many states have significantly reformed or abolished the common-law RAP or allow parties to opt out of the rule in drafting a will or trust if they chose to do so.
    - **Motivations:** Federal tax advantages to dynasty trusts, a jurisdictional competition to attract trust business by allowing trust settlors to skirt around the RAP (at least among states that do not tax income from trust funds).
        - Furthermore, some testators still want to exercise control over the future.

THE PROBLEM OF DEAD HAND CONTROL

- **Generally illustrates the age-old fight between present interests and future interests.**
- **Testators:** Will worry about unwise decisions by the donee, or the testator would like to condition or control the resources into the future.
- **Devisees:** Keeping property and subjecting it to post-mortem control is costly to the owner in that she cannot sell for a price that would reflect future use, or give it away in some other way.

C: MEDIATING CONFLICTS BETWEEN CONCURRENT OWNERS

In co-ownership, the effects of the use by each co-owner are only partially internalized to that owner. That is why in many situations, co-owners need some governance scheme, such as a contract or, more usually, a set of norms of proper use, to regulate and take care of the property.

- Legal solutions take two forms: (1) Afford co-owners exit from the relationship. This is achieved primarily by the action for partition. (2) More detailed governance rules.
- In many American jurisdictions, holders of concurrent interests are quite limited in the remedies available to them, and co-owners in some jurisdictions often wind up seeking an accounting in a partition.

CONCURRENT AND MARITAL ESTATES

- Property can be divided in two dimensions at any given moment in time – **horizontal** and **vertical.**

- Each estate in land defined in terms of temporal duration – fee simple, life estate, remainder, etc. – can be divided among concurrent owners. **Thus, one can create concurrent ownership in a fee simple, concurrent life estates (lasting until the last life tenant dies), and concurrent remainders or executory interests.**
- If there is a partnership, the partnership as an entity holds title to the property, much the way that corporations as entities hold title to property.
    - Under this theory, **there is only one owner of the property – the entity (partnership or corporation) – and issues about who manages and controls the property are resolved as a matter of partnership or corporation law, NOT property law.**
    - Forming a trust, partnership, or corporation is an alternative to the co-ownership arrangements considered here.

Main forms of co-ownership: Tenancy in common, joint tenancy, tenancy by the entirety.

- **Tenancy in common (TIC):** Each tenant has a **separate but undivided interest.**
    - **Separate** in the sense that it is independently descendible, conveyable, and devisable.
        - **Each tenant can unilaterally convey her interest to a third party** – property held as tenancy in common can be attached by creditors of each individual tenant.
        - **No right of survivorship.**
    - **Undivided:** Each tenant in common has the right to possess the whole of the property (although they need not exercise that right). No requirement that each cotenant possess an equal share. Respective obligations to contribute to the payment of taxes or mortgage obligations will be determined by their respective percentage ownership.
- **Joint Tenancy (JT):** Exactly like the tenancy in common, except for the treatment of survivorship. Each joint tenant has a separate and undivided interest. Because the interest is undivided, each joint tenant has the right to possess the whole. **The principal difference is that in a joint tenancy, a surviving joint tenant automatically acquires the interest of another joint tenant when the other tenant dies.**
    - **Requires four unities at the time of creation:**
        - **TIME:** Each interest must be acquired or vest at the same time.
        - **TITLE:** Each must acquire title by the same instrument or by joint adverse possession, never by intestate succession or other act of law.
        - **INTEREST:** Each must have the same legal interest in the property, such as fee simple, life estate, lease, etc., although not necessarily identical fractional shares.
        - **POSSESSION:** Each must have the *right* to possess the whole.
    - **By contrast, the only unity required to create a tenancy in common is that of possession.**
- **Tenancy by the entirety (TBE):** Only exists in a minority of states nowadays, and is **only available for married couples.** In some states that recognize the tenancy by the entirety, **neither spouse can unilaterally transfer or encumber their share of the property without the consent of the other.**

- In all states that recognize this tenancy, there is no UNILATERAL exit option so long as the couple stays married. Both spouses can convey to a "straw" and then have the straw convey back to them as tenants in common, but neither spouse acting on his or her own can sever the tenancy, other than by getting a divorce.
- At common law, a joint tenancy was presumed in any conveyance that satisfied the four unities. Today, a tenancy in common is generally presumed unless there is some other manifestation of intent to create a joint tenancy or a tenancy by the entirety.
    - **Examples:** O conveys "to A and B" – presumed to be tenancy in common.
        - To create a joint tenancy, O would have to say something like "to A and B as joint tenants with right of survivorship and not as tenants in common."
    - Some courts still presume a joint tenancy is intended in case of an ambiguous transfer to a married couple, and states that still recognize **TBE** will presume that this is intended in the case of an ambiguous transfer to a married couple, at least for interests in land.
- **Deciding which arrangement works best:** Influenced by many factors.
    - (1): Survivorship feature in the joint tenancy or the tenancy by the entirety allows a remaining owner to avoid probate. Survivor can sell the property immediately after he or she so chooses.
    - (2): Depending on the rules in place in a given state, the joint tenancy (and even more so the tenancy by the entirety) may afford some protection of jointly owned assets from creditors of one of the co-owners.
    - (3): Finally, tax considerations may come into play.
- **Community Property:** Used in some states of the South and West, esp. those with some Spanish or French law in their early histories.
    - Under this system, all property acquired during the marriage (with exceptions for gifts and bequests to one spouse) automatically becomes community property. Property acquired before the marriage is theoretically separate but may become community property through commingling with community property.
    - On divorce, the spouse arguing that property is separate has the burden of proof and must be able to trace the property.

SEVERANCE
- *Harms v. Sprague* (Four Unities issue): Harms and his brother had a joint tenancy on a piece of land. During his life, the brother issued a mortgage on the land.
    - Questions:
        - (1) Is a joint tenancy severed when fewer than all the joint tenants mortgage their interest in the property?
        - (2) Does such a mortgage survive the death of the mortgagor as a lien?
    - Holding: A JT is not severed when fewer than all the joint tenants mortgage their interest in the property, since it does not disrupt the four unities. The mortgage does not survive the death of the mortgagor.
        - The four unities are: (1) time, (2) title, (3) interest, (4) possession.
        - Since the lien doesn't actually do anything to the joint tenancy, once Harms' brother dies, Harms gets the entire property.

- This is a characteristic of the joint tenancy: each party is entitled to possess the entire property.
    - The lien is attached to Harm's brother's interest in the property. Since his interest dies when he does, the lien does not survive the death of death of Harms' brother.

PARTITION

- ***Delfino v. Vealencis***: Plaintiff and defendant tenants in common. Defendant owned 45/144 interest and occupied a dwelling on the land, and used some of the land for a garbage removal business. No party in possession of remainder. Plaintiffs sought partition by sale, defendant sought partition in kind.
    - Holding:
        - Partition in kind is preferred.
        - Partition by sale only when two conditions met:
            - **(1)** Physical attributes of the land make in-kind partition impracticable or inequitable (e.g. if part of the land was mountains). **AND**
            - **(2)** Interests of all parties would be better promoted by sale.
        - Here, the land was rectangular and easily divisible, and defendant faced possibility of losing her home and business if the land was sold. **Therefore, partition in kind.**
    - **Note 2:** In theory, one co-owner can always buy out the other co-owners. However, **nature of TIC means that bilateral monopolies/holdout behavior might be created.**
    - **Note 3:** Courts have increasingly favored partition by sale. In a partition in kind, courts will try if possible to allow a cotenant living on the parcel to keep the portion on which she lives.
        - **Reasons for this:** Partition in kind creates huge administrative burden on the court to determine the exact division of the parcel (no such issue in partition by sale).

OUSTER

- ***Gillmor v. Gillmor***: 2 brothers own land and eventually die leaving to heirs, including plaintiff and defendant, as TIC. Plaintiff sought damages and partition because defendant was exclusively using land (grazing) and refused to let the plaintiff use the land to graze.
    - Holding:
        - Mere exclusive use of land is not enough for ouster.
            - **Land must be used such that it necessarily excludes a cotenant and prevents that cotenant from exercising his rights in the property.**
                - Satisfied here because defendant's actions prevented any use by plaintiff.
        - General rule is that tenants out of possession aren't entitled to rent from tenants in possession except if tenant in possession ousts.
            - **Minority rule is that you have to pay even without ouster.**
            - **Justifications:** Put land to good use, could spur cotenants into seeking partition.
    - Ouster can be a basis to claim title under adverse possession.
    - Ouster can be a justification for the payment of rent.

- o **Repairs and improvements:** When cotenant makes repairs or improvements to the common property w/o consent of his fellow cotenants, <u>he generally has no right of contribution.</u>
  - Cotenant may be required to contribute his pro rata share of expenses if the cotenant in possession <u>(1)</u> acted in good faith, <u>(2)</u> With the bona fide belief that he was the sole owner of the property, or <u>(3)</u> when the repairs were essential to preserve or protect the common estate.
- o **Note 1:** If one cotenant <u>rents to a third party</u>, then the renting cotenant is obliged to share the payments with other cotenants.

MARITAL INTERESTS

- *O'Brien v. O'Brien*: Husband and wife get divorced. During the marriage, wife contributed to the husband's medical school costs. Upon divorce, wife wanted to get some of the enhanced earnings which her ex-husband would derive from his medical practice.
  - o **Holding:** Enhanced earnings are considered property for the purpose of settling a divorce. Court asked three questions:
    - (1) Should the wife get some compensation for her contributions to her husband's acquisition of the medical license?
      - Return on investment theory, very popular in the 1980s
      - Unjust enrichment/restitution rationale.
      - Compensation because the wife was harmed by giving up her own opportunities. Put her in the position if she hadn't been harmed in this way.
      - Key argument <u>against</u> compensation is that the degree was a product of his efforts. Any enhanced earnings would also be a product of his labor.
    - (2) How should she be compensated? Property or maintenance?
      - The court seems fixated on creating marital property, ignoring the idea of maintenance (formerly called alimony).
        - Here, the court is rejecting the liability protection, and granting property protection (Calabresi distinction).
        - Upon divorce, you don't just separate out the property, you also need child support and maintenance.
        - The court ignores maintenance is that in the 1970s and 1980s it was regard very poorly, particularly by feminists. We want a clear break because marriage is an economic arrangement anyway. Maintenance perpetuates the relationship and doesn't allow for a clear break.

      Advantages of the property route?
        - Maintenance ends on remarriage, so we're concerned about complete compensation.
          - o Might be easier to enforce (although in this case, the court sort of comes up with a distribution scheme of the property right that looks a lot like maintenance).

      Disadvantages of the property route?
        - The certainty of the paying spouse means that they have to pay no matter what circumstances arise.
        - Values of the property might change over time.

- Lot of assumptions in the valuations (e.g. that husband will stay in one medical specialty).

(3) How much should she be compensated?
Have to decide this no matter if you like property rights or maintenance rights.
How does the court come up on their 40% value?
- The length of the marriage
- The current value is more like 10-15%.

VI: Entity Property: Separating Management and Possession

A: THE LEASE AND LANDLORD-TENANT LAW

- The forms of property considered in the last section **largely reflect an exclusion strategy for dealing with resources, rather than a governance strategy.**
- In order to provide for more effective management of resources in these settings, **the law has developed certain devices that effectively allow owners to switch to a governance strategy for the management of resources. These devices can be termed "ENTITY PROPERTY"**
- **Distinction between devices whose function is to govern multiple *possessory* interests in the use of a single complex of assets, and devices whose function is to govern multiple *nonpossessory* interests in the enjoyment of assets.**
- PRINCIPAL DEVICES (in the former category): **Leases, co-operatives, and condominiums.**

SEPARATING MANAGEMENT AND POSSESSORY RIGHTS

- Leases are more attractive to those who cannot or do not want to invest their own resources in the larger enterprise. Co-ops and condos are more attractive to those who do not want to make such an investment (either for tax or other reasons).

1. **Leases:** Also known as LEASEHOLDS, TENANCIES, the TERM OF YEARS, or LANDLORD-TENANT INTERESTS. **The terms are basically interchangeable.**
   - Can be thought of as another form of property, like the fee simple, life estate, and defeasible fees.
   - **Leases have always been regarded as somewhat different from the other forms.**
     - This reflects the fact that the landlord typically plays a much more active role in the governance of the underlying assets than do persons who hold future interests under traditional freehold interests in property – e.g. reversions, remainders, possibility of reverter.
   - **Reasons for enduring appeal of leases** – Three aspects:
     - **1: Leases are a de facto financing device.** One can think of a lease as an arrangement in which the owner of the property lends possession to another, in exchange for periodic payments of money called rent.
       - Original function of leases was to avoid prohibition on usury.
       - **Rent charge includes an interest component, reflecting the time value of money and the anticipated rate of inflation.**
       - Appealing because persons who have not accumulated much in the way of assets or have poor credit will prefer to lease assets rather than purchase them.

- Leases allow people to <u>leverage their limited resources in roughly the same way that borrowing allows persons to leverage limited resources.</u>
    - **2. Leases operate as a risk-spreading device:** Renting is a way of minimizing the risks of investing most of one's savings in an asset that one may want to unload in fairly short order (and an asset whose risk may be tightly correlated with one's employment risk).
        - <u>For landlords, leasing can be a risk-spreading device as well.</u> If tenant defaults on the rental obligation, it is usually easier to retake possession of the property than it is to foreclose on a mortgage and retake property held as security for a loan.
        - Built-in security interest provided by leases and the ability to spread risks among multiple leaseholders have long made leasing of property a popular form of investment.
    - **3: Leases operate as a mechanism for integrating and managing complexes of assets, and in that sense function as a kind of entity property.**
        - Leasing allows owners of resources to switch from a simple exclusion strategy to a governance strategy in overcoming various coordination problems.
            - **Example:** Leases allow complexes of assets to be managed using a governance strategy, characterized by a specialization of functions. In a shopping center, for example, the landlord can build, maintain and insure the parking lot, utility systems, common walkways, and can even provide marketing for the complex as a whole.
                - <u>Both the common areas and the individual retail spaces are probably managed more effectively and with lower transaction costs because of this specialization of functions.</u>
    - **Problem with leases:** One body of legal doctrine has been developed that must accommodate both simple leases used as financing or risk-spreading devices, and complex leases used to provide governance structures for complicated enterprises serving multiple persons.
        - <u>L-T law was formed during an era when leases were simple and were largely used as financing and risk-spreading devices</u>, with the agricultural lease being the central example.

LEASE TYPES
- <u>Term of Years:</u> This refers to a lease that has a fixed time at which it terminates or ends. Usually this is for one or more years (hence the name), but it can be for a shorter time. **Leases for any term longer than one year must be in writing, per the Statute of Frauds.**
    - <u>Neither the landlord nor the tenant is required to give notice to the other before terminating the relationship.</u>
- <u>Periodic tenancy:</u> This refers to a lease that automatically rolls over for a stated period of time, usually a year or a month. For example, a lease from year to year is a periodic tenancy that automatically rolls over one year at a time.

- o In contrast to the term of years, a <u>periodic tenancy requires that each of the parties give notice to the other if they desire to terminate the lease. Usually, the notice period is the same as the period of recurring rollover.</u>
- **Tenancy at will:** This refers to a tenancy that lasts only so long as both parties wish it to continue. Either party can terminate at any time for any reason.
    - o <u>**At common law, no notice was required for termination of a tenancy at will.**</u> This has been changed in many jurisdictions to require notice equal to the period of time at which rent payments are made.
- **Tenancy at sufferance:** This refers to the situation in which an individual who was once in rightful possession of property holds over after this right has ended. <u>**A tenant at sufferance differs from a trespasser in that the tenant's original entry was not wrongful.**</u> In many jurisdictions, this difference may limit the landlord's ability to use self-help to evict the tenant at sufferance. Otherwise, the landlord is free to evict the tenant at sufferance using forcible entry and detainer statutes, or by bringing an action in ejectment.
- Limited menu of leases is another example of the ***numerus clausus*** principle.

THE INDEPENDENT COVENANTS MODEL (Historic Period)
- <u>Central assumption</u> was that the lease was at heart a conveyance of a possessory interest in property. The possessory right – including the right to exclude others from the asset – was transferred from the landlord to the tenant for the prescribed term of the lease.
- *Paradine v. Jane:* Reflects the view that a lease is <u>a conveyance of an interest in land, but it also reflects the view that a lease is a contract – a bundle of covenants or promises, some running from L to T and some running from T to L.</u>
    - o Most important covenant: <u>The covenant of quiet enjoyment – A promise not to interfere with the tenant's possession of the land during the term of the lease.</u>
    - o Leading example of the <u>independent covenants model of the L-T relationship</u>.
- **Key structure of independent covenants model:** All covenants must be performed without regard to whether other covenants have been or can be performed.
    - o <u>Even if landlord fails to perform a covenant, such as a covenant to repair the premises, the tenant must continue to perform the covenant to pay rent.</u>
    - o <u>If tenant fails to perform the covenant to pay rent, the landlord must continue to perform the covenant of quiet possession.</u>
    - o <u>Remedy in all these events is for the aggrieved party to sue for breach of covenant.</u>
- <u>Under independent covenants model, the allocation of risk under a lease is entirely on the tenant.</u> The tenant captures any economic gains and losses associated with the property during the terms of the lease.
    - o If the property that was the subject of the lease was destroyed or damaged, the tenant's obligation to pay rent continues uninterrupted. <u>Over time, this specific application of the allocation of risk gradually was changed by legislation.</u>
- *Smith v. McEnany:* Gives good overview of the <u>doctrine of partial eviction.</u>
    - o Doctrine of partial eviction in *Smith:* A wrongful eviction of the tenant (<u>whether partially or wholly</u>) by the landlord from part of the premises suspends the rent under the lease.

- o **Modern approach to partial eviction (following mode of dependent covenants):** Per the *Restatement*, in a case of a partial eviction the tenant should be given a choice either to terminate the lease or to continue the lease as to the part from which the tenant has not been evicted with a claim for damages or abatement of rent for the part lost to eviction.
- o <u>Rule does not apply to a de minimis encroachment.</u>

DUTY TO DELIVER POSSESSION
- If tenant cannot take possession because the landlord is still in possession, or because a third party acting under a paramount title given by the landlord (e.g. a previous tenant whose lease has not expired) is still in possession, then <u>the covenant of quiet enjoyment means that the landlord guarantees the tenant will be able to take possession of the property when the lease begins.</u>
- If a squatter or holdover tenant is in possession, then the authorities are divided:
  - o **English rule:** Landlord is responsible for clearing out any squatters or holdover tenants at the beginning of the lease.
  - o **American rule:** Tenant is responsible for getting rid of any squatters or holdover tenants.
    - ▪ Either way, parties can modify the rule by drafting appropriate lease clause.
- *Best default rule:* The one we think most landlords and tenants would agree upon if they had the foresight to consider the issue when negotiating the lease.
  - o Assuming that both parties are fully informed about the relevant variables, <u>the rule they would adopt would plausibly be the one that assigns the duty to the party who is best able to detect the presence of squatters or holdover tenants and to bring actions to have them evicted before the lease starts.</u>
    - ▪ In the context of rentals of urban apartments, <u>this is almost surely the landlord.</u>
    - ▪ In other circumstances, <u>the tenant may be the cheaper evictor</u> (e.g. lease of rural agricultural land where landlord is an absentee owner).
    - ▪ Best idea might be to have different packages of default rules for different types of leases.
- *Sutton v. Temple:* Defendant leased a field to graze cattle. Cattle died. Cause was poisonous paint embedded in the soil throughout the field. Plaintiff was not aware of the state of the field at the time of leasing. Plaintiff sued defendant for unpaid rent.
  - o **Holding:** <u>No implied warranty of fitness for intended purpose – defendant was liable for paying the rent for the land even though he could not use it.</u>
  - o **General Rule:** When a man undertakes to pay a specific rent for a piece of land, he is obliged to pay that rent, whether it is fit for the intended purpose for which he took it or not.
  - o **Rationale:** <u>Doctrine of independent covenants, allocation of risk on the tenant rather than the landlord</u> (since tenant was theoretically in a better position to inspect the land and determine whether or not it was fit for the intended use).
    - ▪ Importantly, there was no supposed fraud on the part of the plaintiff.

- o Case illustrates the doctrine of **caveat lessee** (tenant beware) in its pure and harsh form. **No implied warranty that the leased premises would be fit for the tenant's intended purposes.**
- o Judges went to great pains to distinguish *Smith v. Marrable*, where it was held that there was an implied warranty of fitness for intended purpose on the rental of a furnished vacation cottage.
  - Rationale for holding in *Smith v. Marrable*: Value of the rental was mostly in the furniture.
- o Courts continued to assume that rentals of unfurnished apartments were governed by the rule of *cavat lessee* until the late 1960s and early 1970s.

EXTENSION OF THE INDEPENDENT COVENANTS MODEL (Transitional Period)

- **Forfeiture clauses:** Clauses in leases, insisted upon by landlords, providing that upon the tenant's violation of enumerated covenants in the lease – most crucially the covenant to pay rent – the tenant's interest in the lease would be immediately forfeited.
  - o **Two forms (both modeled after defeasible fees):** (1) Analogous to the fee simple determinable, the lease forfeits automatically upon violation of specified covenants by the tenant. (2) Analogous to the fee simple subject to condition subsequent, the violation of specific covenants by the tenant authorizes the landlord to "re-enter and re-take" the premises.
  - o **Clauses are generally upheld by the courts. They in effect convert the specified tenant covenants covered by the forfeiture clause from independent covenants into dependent covenants.**
  - o With addition of an enforceable forfeiture clause, the tenant's failure to pay rent means that the tenant's interest in the leasehold estate is subject to forfeiture, in effect releasing the landlord from the covenant of quiet enjoyment.
  - o **Clauses transformed the lease into a bundle of covenants that were independent insofar as the promises ran to the tenant, and dependent insofar as the promises ran to the landlord.**
- *Blackett v. Olanoff:* Tenants' implied warranty of quiet enjoyment was violated by late evening and early morning music and disturbances coming from nearby premises which the landlords leased to others for use as a bar or cocktail lounge. **Tenants were constructively evicted.**
  - o **Constructive eviction rule:** Based on the exception to independent covenants recognized for actual evictions by the landlord. **Substantial interference by the landlord (misfeasance or nonfeasance) for a substantial time which results in an actual vacation of the premises is a constructive eviction.** This excuses the tenant from further payment of rent.
    - **Landlord nonfeasance rather than misfeasance:** Landlords can be held responsible for constructive eviction based on nonfeasance.
      - **Rationales:** One theory for holding a landlord responsible for constructive eviction based on nonfeasance turns on whether the landlord's inaction violates some specific clause in the tenant's lease. This was the case here in *Blackett.*

- It is generally required that the tenant vacate the premises before it can bring a suit for constructive eviction.
  - Tenant must generally vacate the premises within a reasonable time.
- There are some precedents upholding claims for partial constructive eviction.
- *Gotleib v. Taco Bell Corp.:* This case outlines the doctrine of repudiation and surrender of a lease.
  - Landlord's options when a lessee attempts to repudiate a lease prior to its expiration:
    - (1) Landlord may reject the repudiation and do nothing. If the landlord does so, the tenant continues to remain liable under the terms of the lease.
      - No obligation for a commercial lessor (landlord) to mitigate damages.
      - Obligation to mitigate damages is imposed on residential landlords.
    - (2) Lessor can enter the premises and re-let them as the tenant's agent for its own benefit. In this case, the tenant remains liable for any rent deficiency.
      - Tenant is also liable for full rent during period it takes for landlord to find new tenant, + any reasonable expenditures in finding a new tenant (e.g. cost of advertisements).
    - (3) The lessor also has the option to accept the repudiation, re-enter the premises and re-let for its own benefit. In that event the lessee is generally relieved from any further liability under the lease. No further rent accrues because the L-T relationship no longer exists.
      - Lessors will attempt to hybridize option (2) and (3). They will try to stay in option (2) for as long as possible to keep the lessee liable for rent, then move to option (3) as soon as they find a new tenant.
        - Counter: Most leases signed significantly before move in so hybrid is impractical because Lessor would lose time between signing of new lease and new lease beginning.
  - When is a repudiation accepted?
    - By express agreement.
    - By operation of law – when it is inferred from the conduct of the parties.
      - Acceptance of a surrender is created by operation of law when the parties to a lease do some act so inconsistent with the L-T relationship which implies "their intent to deem the lease terminated."
      - An outward refusal to accept repudiation of the lease does not bar a finding that the subsequent conduct of the parties creates an acceptance by operation of law.
      - Mere attempts to re-let the premises are insufficient to establish an acceptance by operation of law.
        - Detail and degree of plaintiffs' actions (written offer to Rite-Aid for their sole benefit) went above "mere attempts."
        - Payment of lesser amounts of rent, delivery of keys not enough under lease here

- Once repudiation is accepted, then former tenant is liable for the full amount of rent owed up to the moment of acceptance, BUT IS OFF THE HOOK THEREAFTER.
  - Notes:
    - **(1):** Doctrine of surrender, like doctrine of constructive eviction, is pro-tenant.
      - Surrender doctrine emerged as courts reasoned that Ls and Ts could create a mutual release by *implied contract*. This would happen if the tenant vacated the premises with the intention never to return, in effect making an offer to surrender.
      - Offer and acceptance of the surrender of the lease do not have to be in writing, Statute of Frauds notwithstanding.
    - **(2):** Landlord's state of mind must be to "accept" the abandonment and reclaim the leasehold interest as an entitlement belonging to the landlord.
      - **Clear acceptance:** Landlord changes the locks (thus excluding the tenant from further possession), or re-lets to a third party.
      - **Less clear:** Retaining the keys after they have been dropped off by the tenant or entering the premises to put up a "For Rent" sign.
    - **(3):** Under the option in which the landlord acts as the abandoning tenant's agent, the landlord can seek a new tenant and sue the abandoning tenant for damages equal to any benefit of the bargain under the original lease.
      - For example, if the landlord re-enters and advertises the premises, but three months go by before a suitable substitute tenant is found, the original tenant will remain liable for an additional three months' rent (in addition to any unpaid rent up to the time of abandonment).
    - **(4): Rent acceleration clauses.** Under these, in the event of a tenant default, all the rent owing under the lease is made immediately due. Courts have tended to take a dim view of these clauses, perhaps influenced by the traditional understanding that "the rent issues out of the land"
      - As courts have begun to treat leases more like bilateral contracts, acceleration clauses have been viewed with less hostility, although usually on the understanding that the landlord has a duty to mitigate damages under such a clause. Some jurisdictions continue to refuse to enforce acceleration clauses if they are deemed to be an excessive liquidated damages penalty.

THE MODEL OF DEPENDENT COVENANTS (Modern Era)
- The 1970s witnessed a revolution in L-T law, characterized as entailing the repudiation of a property conception of leases in favor of a contract model of leases.
- A more accurate characterization might be that the contractual aspect of landlord-tenant law moved decisively away from the model of independent covenants, toward the model of dependent covenants.
- *Sommer v. Kridel:* Residential landlord has obligation to make reasonable efforts to MITIGATE DAMAGES if property is wrongfully vacated by a tenant.

- o No standard formula for determining whether the landlord has utilized satisfactory efforts in attempting to mitigate damages. Each case must be judged upon its own facts.
- o **Note 2:** 42 states and DC have adopted the duty to mitigate damages when the tenant abandons, at least for residential leases. The duty to mitigate is a pure contract doctrine.

ASSIGNMENT AND SUBLEASE

- Two types of transfers of tenant interests – <u>sublease and assignment</u>.
- **Sublease:** Operates much like subinfeudation. L starts out with a fee simple, the landlord carves out a lease for the prime tenant from the fee simple, then the prime tenant carves out a sublease for the subtenant from the prime lease, and so on and so forth.
- **Assignment:** Operates much like alienation. L starts with a fee simple, the landlord carves out a lease for the prime tenant from the fee simple, then the prime tenant alienates the prime lease to a first assignee, then the first assignee alienates the prime lease to a second assignee, and so forth. <u>The prime lease as a whole is transferred to successive assignees, each of which then steps into the shoes of her assignor.</u>
- **Distinction:** The distinction is important because it affects who the landlord and the tenant in possession must deal with when problems arise in the ongoing relationship under the lease.
  - o **Sublease:** Like a feudal hierarchy – the landlord deals with the prime lessee, who deals with the subtenant. Each chain in the hierarchy has its own separate lease (sublease, sub-sublease, etc) that defines the rights and obligations between the particular pair of parties to that instrument.
  - o **Assignment:** The assignee steps into the shoes of the prime tenant, and as such enters into direct relations with the original landlord. <u>After a series of assignments, there are still only two parties who deal with the property, the original landlord and the latest assignee.</u>
- Two sources of L-T obligation: **Privity of estate and privity of contract.**
  - o **Privity of contract:** The obligations that derive from privity of contract are just those which come from being a party to a binding bilateral contract (in this case, a lease). If the original landlord and the prime tenant enter into a lease, <u>they are both bound by privity of contract.</u> If the landlord and the subtenant have not entered into any contractual relationship with one another, they are not bound by privity of contract.
  - o **Privity of estate:** Two conditions must be met for privity of estate to apply: (1) The parties to be bound must have interests such that one is directly carved out of the interest of the other. <u>One might say that the parties must have interests that are directly "nested" with one another.</u> (2) One of the parties must be in actual possession of the property or have a reversion. If these conditions are satisfied, then the parties are bound by privity of estate in addition to privity of contract.
  - o Prime tenant subleases to subtenant & subtenant in possession, then <u>the prime tenant is in privity of estate with the subtenant, and the subtenant with the prime tenant.</u> However, <u>the original landlord is not in privity of estate with the subtenant, nor is the subtenant in privity of estate with the original landlord, because the tenant's interest is not carved directly out of the landlord's interest.</u>

- Distinction is most important when considering assignments. On the sublease side of things, privity of contract and privity of estate cover exactly the same people.
    - **Assignments:** The assignee does not destroy the contractual relationship between the prime tenant and the landlord – **they are still in privity of contract.** However, there is no contractual relationship between the original landlord and the first assignee, and so there is no privity of contract between the original landlord and the first assignee. However, <u>the first assignee has now stepped into the shoes of the prime tenant and holds an interest – the prime leasehold interest – that is directly carved out of the landlord's interest, and the first assignee is not in possession of the property. Therefore, the original landlord and the first assignee are in privity of estate.</u>
    - When two parties are in privity of estate, but **NOT** privity of contract, <u>we look to the lease that defines the original leasehold interest, and we impose on the parties those covenants that run with the land.</u> The covenants which run with the land are those which **"touch and concern" the land.**
    - **Which is better if you are a landlord?** It depends on how active you are in managing the property. If you are inactive, you may prefer a sublease, because now the prime tenant will serve as the landlord to the subtenant. If you are actively involved in management, an assignment is probably better. <u>With an assignment, the tenant in possession owes a duty to pay rent and perform other obligations that run with the land directly to you under privity of estate.</u>
        - The prime tenant serves as a surety for the performance of obligations by the assignee, as it were.
- **Assumption and novation:**
    - <u>Assumption:</u> Occurs if the first assignee expressly agrees as part of an assignment agreement to be bound by the terms of the original lease. In effect, <u>when an assignee makes an assumption, the assignee contractually agrees to be bound by privity of contract as well as by privity of estate.</u>
        - If assignment with assumption, the prime tenant is still bound by privity of contract, meaning that there are now two parties bound by privity of contract.
    - <u>Novation:</u> Occurs when the parties agree to erase any privity of contract liability on the part of the prime tenant.
- *Kendall v. Ernest Pestana, Inc:* Consent to assign a commercial lease, where a lease provides for assignment only with the prior consent of the lessor, can only be withheld when the lessor has a commercially reasonable objection to the assignee or the proposed use.
    - Applies even in the absence of a provision in the lease stating that consent to assignment will not be unreasonably withheld.
    - Denying consent solely on basis of personal taste, convenience, or sensibility is NOT commercially reasonable
    - **Court's Rationale.** Adopts the minority rule:
        - (1) The law generally favors the free alienation of property.

- (2) Treating leases as contracts imports the implied duty of good faith, which requires commercially reasonable objection.
- (3) Common-law reason (majority rule) doesn't hold because L-T relationship is less personal than before.
- **Factors:** financial responsibility, suitability, legality, need for alteration, nature of occupancy, etc...
- **Dissent Counter:** Minority rule will lead to unnecessary litigation
  - **Majority Rule:** When lease contains an approval clause, consent can be withheld for any reason. (Rejected by this Court, recognized by dissent)
    - Majority Rule Justifications:
      - Lease is an interest in real property (Court objects because lease is contract)
      - Approval clause is unambiguous reservation of power
      - Stare decisis in favor of majority rule.
      - Increases in value belong to the lessor not the lessee

Both majority and minority rules are default rules – parties can contract out of them.

The result of this ruling is that there is a one time windfall to lessees, and the expected outcome is that landlords will now either contract out of this rule, or try to compensate themselves by increasing rent.

Note 1: Economically speaking, issue in this case is which party (L or T) is entitled to capture the bonus value under the terms of the prime lease.

Airbnb

There are six lease agreement amendment proposals:
- Tenant bears liability for any fines or violations incurred- this type helps protect against the chance that the STR (short-term rental) is deemed illegal by the local authorities.
- Landlord will receive a set percentage of profits gained- allows landlord to get paid when others reside on the property and state why it's a reasonable expectation. Can set it high enough to deter people from allowing
- Tenant is required to provide written advance notice- you have an interest in knowing when someone else will be occupying a space in your building and it will give you adequate warning.
- Tenant agrees to purchase extra liability insurance- insurance to cover any serious property damage, may do this based on the amount of renter traffic.
- Tenant must pay an additional security deposit- security deposit just to cover the added risk of damage
- Landlord shall be able to pre-screen STR tenants- allow yourself to have right to refuse any rental for added security and to screen STRs.

CONDITION OF THE PREMISES
- *Javins v. First National Realty Corp*: Tenants had not paid their rent, alleging numerous violations of the Housing Regulations (about 1500 violations).
  - **Holding:** Court found an <u>implied warranty of habitability in residential leases.</u>

- Tenant's obligation to pay rent is **dependent on the landlord's performance of his obligations, including the IWH.**
    - If IWH is breached, then tenant's obligation to pay rent is partially or wholly suspended.
- **IWH is nonwaivable – cannot contract out of it.**
- Determination of whether or not IWH is breached **depends on whether the housing code has been breached.** One or two minor violations of the housing code standing alone are de minimis, and do not breach the IWH.
- Overturns *caveat lessee* – the idea that there is no implied warranty that land is suitable for tenant's use.
- Rationale for holding:
    - **(1)** Old rule (caveat lessee) was based on assumption that land was the most important part of a leasehold. This assumption was no longer correct today – **for urban tenants, most important part of the leasehold is the dwelling, not the land beneath the dwelling.**
        - Tenants also do not have specialized knowledge or tools needed to make all but basic repairs to their dwellings.
    - **(2)** Landlord is the **cheapest cost avoider** – landlord has much greater opportunity, incentive, and capacity to inspect and maintain the condition of his buildings.
    - **(3)** Unequal bargaining power between landlords and tenants (landlord deals with tenants individually, high organizational costs if tenants were to try and organize).
    - **(4)** Idea that **poor housing is detrimental to the whole of society.**
- **Note 2-3:** IWH is one of several residential L-T law reforms introduced during the transitional period. THe other two of note are the **doctrine of retaliatory eviction** and the **illegal lease doctrine:**
    - **Doctrine of retaliatory eviction:** Landlord may not retaliate against a tenant for reporting code violations.
        - Only affects small subset of tenants (e.g. tenants' union activists).
    - Illegal lease doctrine: If, **at the time of leasing (when lease is executed)**, the property is subject to one or more code violations, then the lease is void and has no legal effect (meaning that landlord cannot sue for unpaid rent based on the lease).
        - Not popular since **tenant cannot claim the benefit of the lease either (including the covenant of quiet enjoyment).** This means that Landlord could immediately begin eviction proceedings.
        - By contrast, IWH gives the tenant additional rights under the lease w/o subjecting the tenant to immediate eviction.
- **Note 4: No implied warranty of fitness in commercial cases (except in very small minority of states).**
- **Note 5:** Most common rationale for making the IWH a mandatory rule of law is the perception that tenants and landlords have unequal bargaining power.

- o **Note 6:** <u>Either the municipal housing code or community standards can serve as a means for defining the content of the IWH.</u>
- o **Note 7:** The doctrine of constructive eviction continues to play a role in jurisdictions that have adopted the IWH (since most have only adopted the IWH for residential leases). <u>When issues related to commercial leases arise, they continue to be addressed using the doctrine of constructive eviction</u>
  - ▪ Constructive eviction may also be relevant under residential leases.
- o **Note 8:** Remedies for violation of IWH include **(1)** Rescission of the lease; **(2)** Specific performance of the IWH; **(3)** Action for damages; **(4)** Set-off against rent liability reflecting the violation of the IWH; **(5)** In some jurisdictions, withholding of rent until the landlord corrects the violations.
  - ▪ Standard formula for determining damages (taking rent reserved under the lease and subtracting the value of the premises in their noncompliant condition) often yields 0 damage.
  - ▪ <u>Substitute formulas:</u> **(1)** Fair market value if premises were IWH compliant; **(2)** Percentage reduction.

CONSEQUENCES OF IWH
Economics of L-T Reform
- By making this implied warranty of habitability, it could increase the demand of low-cost housing (because product will be better) and increase costs of supplying such housing (because compliance would cost landlords money).
- However, some argue that low-income rental market is different from other types of product markets in that the "market" of people can't afford higher prices so prices might not necessarily go up because they're incapable of paying more.

B. Co-Ops, Condos, and Common-Interest Communities
- Three alternative forms of entity property – property in which multiple persons enjoy individual possessory interests while common areas are subject to specialized management: **Condominiums, Co-operatives, Association Subdivision.**
- Individual possessory rights in these three are functionally equivalent to a fee simple – **these property forms are not used as financing or risk spreading devices like leases are.**
  - o Only encountered in contexts where separation of management functions of common areas from individual possessory units is desired.
- **Co-op:** Legally speaking, a co-op is a corporation. The corporation holds fee simple title to the entire complex, including both the individual units (typically apartments) and the common facilities.
  - o Individuals who wish to live in the building must purchase shares of stock in the corporation, and the corporation then leases a designated space to them, typically under a long-term renewable lease of 99 years.
  - o Common areas are owned and managed by the corporation, acting through a board of directors elected by the shareholders. <u>Individual shareholders are responsible for paying the debt on the building.</u>

- For this reason, co-ops have historically been rather picky about creditworthiness of potential shareholders.
- **Condominiums:** Differ from co-ops in that individual units – typically apartments, but also townhouses, are owned within the walls by individuals in fee simple. Common areas are owned by the unit owners as tenants in common.
    - Tenancy in common is regulated by a master deed or declaration which is binding on all unit owners.
        - Master deed typically calls for the creation of a homeowners' association (HOA), which manages the common facilities and charges assessments to the unit owners to pay for the upkeep, operating expenses, and taxes associated with the common facilities.
- **Association Subdivision:** Consists of stand-alone units which nevertheless enjoy certain facilities in common with other stand-alone units.
    - Can be organized as condos or created using servitudes running with the land, or may be formed under special statutes that set forth the basic outlines of their organization and governance.
- Common interest communities represent a kind of democracy, while leases are a form of dictatorship.

CONDOS v. COOPERATIVES
- Co-ops today are mostly confined to NYC.
- Condos command a higher price than do cooperative apartments for otherwise similar units. A recent study finds that the typical condo will sell for 8.8% more than an equivalent co-operative.
- Greater appeal of the condominium is due to two factors:
    - **(1)** Financing.
    - **(2)** Co-op boards typically impose serious financial restrictions on who can buy into a co-op. This limits the number of potential purchasers, which drives down the price.
- Two principal mechanisms are used in co-ops and condos to solve ongoing governance problems: **(1)** The articles of incorporation establishing the condo or coop will contain a number of rules and regulations that run with the ownership of the individual interests; **(2)** Establishment of a HOA (or equivalent) that is charged with authority to establish rules and regulations – and bring enforcement actions – against individual unit owners.
- ***Nahrstedt v. Lakeside Village Condominium Association, Inc.*** **(CA 1994):** Plaintiff purchased a condo in Lakeside CA. Developer's declaration contained a number of covenants, including a covenant that prevented pets in the condo.
    - Ms. Nahrstedt had three cats, and eventually the HOA found out and ordered her to remove the cats and also to pay some fines for violating the covenants.
    - **Holding:** Restrictions in the declaration or master deed are presumed reasonable or valid unless:
        - **(1)** Arbitrary
        - **(2)** Imposes burdens that substantially outweigh benefits to development residents OR

- **(3)** Violates public policy.
  - Restrictions are presumed to be reasonable.
- Reasonableness and unreasonableness should be looked at through the lens of the "common interest development as a whole," rather than the "objecting homeowner"
  - This holding is adopted in part from a case called *Hidden Harbour Estates v. Basso* (Fla. Dist. Ct. App. 1981).
    - In that case, it is also held that restrictions created *after* the creation of the HA should be subject to a standard of "reasonableness."
  - **Rationale for holding: (1)** Provides assurances to prospective condo owners that the covenants in the master declaration will be upheld **(protects reliance interest)**
    - **(2)** Discourages lawsuits by owners of individual units seeking personal exemptions from the restrictions.
      - This protects all owners in the planned development from unanticipated increases in association fees to fund the defense of legal challenges.
  - **Note 5:** Some law and econ scholars have argued that use restrictions contained in the master deed of a complex are presumptively efficient because the developer of the project will have an incentive to include only those restrictions that cause the purchase price of units to go up.
- *40 W. 67th Street v. Pullman*
  - **Business judgment rule:** Common-law doctrine by which courts exercise restraint and defer to good faith decisions made by boards of directors in business settings. **In the context of a co-operative board,** the business judgment rule applies provided that the decisions are:
    - **(1):** Supposed to advance the corporate interest/corporate purpose.
    - **(2):** Are acting within the scope of the co-op's board powers, AND
    - **(3):** Are not in bad faith
    - **The co-op boards have to demonstrate the above in their internal deliberations. The co-op as to have competent evidence, but in deciding whether they have competent evidence, the court will defer to the decision of the co-op board.**
    - If one of these three conditions is not met, courts should undertake review of board decisions.

3 standards of review for common interest community decisions and rules
From most deferential to least deferential:
- **Business judgment rule:** (Levandusky and Pullman NY Ct of Appeals)
  - Court defers to board decisions if board acts.
    - For the purposes of the co-operative.
    - Within the scope of its authority, and
    - In good faith
- **"Un"Reasonableness** (Nahrstedt, Cal. Supreme Ct.)
  - Restriction in the declaration presumed reasonable or valid unless
    - Arbitrary

- Imposes burdens that substantially outweigh benefits to development residents OR
- Violates fundamental public policy.
- **Reasonableness** (Hidden Harbour Estates, Fla. Dist. Ct. App., p. 755)
  - Restrictions added later by board evaluated under reasonableness test.
  - Not presumed valid.
  - To ensure that boards govern to promote "health, happiness, and peace of mind" of project Owners.

VII: The Law of Neighbors

A. NUISANCE
- **Basic Framework:** Traditional starting point is where trespass leaves off.
  - **Trespass:** Controls relatively large intrusions of land.
  - **Nuisance:** Governs <u>lesser intrusions that go only to use and enjoyment.</u>
    - Law of nuisance <u>requires the court to balance the utility of two conflicting uses.</u>
    - Reasonableness of the interference is often an issue. Reasonableness inquiry calls for balancing the value of the competing landowners' activities.
      - <u>An activity is unreasonable if the social harm of the defendant's activity outweighs its social utility.</u>
- *Adams v. Cleveland-Cliffs Iron Co.*: Plaintiffs brought suit in both trespass and nuisance, complaining of dust, noise and vibrations from nearby iron mine. On appeal, defendants raised issue of whether plaintiffs could bring a claim in trespass.
  - **Holding:** No, the plaintiffs could not bring a claim in trespass. Recovery in trespass appropriate for **appreciable** intrusion onto land; recovery in nuisance appropriate for **substantial and unreasonable interference with right to quiet enjoyment.**
  - **Analysis:** Court distinguished trespass and nuisance.
    - Trespass – violates a landowner's right to exclude others from the premises; <u>landholder could recover at least nominal damages even in the absence of proof of other injury.</u>
      - Required that the invasion of the land be **direct or immediate**, and <u>in the form of a physical, tangible object (interfering with exclusive possessory interest).</u>
      - **"Direct invasion requirement"** still alive for trespass in Michigan – for purposes of trespass, direct invasion is one accomplished by any means that the offender knew or reasonably should have known would result in the physical invasion of plaintiff's land.
    - **Nuisance:** Recovery for nuisance traditionally required **(1)** proof of actual and substantial injury; **(2)** test balancing the disturbance complained of against the social utility of its cause.
      - <u>Traditionally required proof of actual and substantial injury.</u>

- Court rejected the "modern doctrine" of permitting recovery in trespass for indirect, intangible invasions that nonetheless interfered with exclusive possessory interest.
  - Court noted that this "grafted onto the law of trespass a requirement of actual and substantial damages" more like nuisance.
- **Noise, dust, and vibrations DO NOT count as tangible objects; cannot give rise to action in trespass.**
  - **Note 1 - Four tests**, singly or in combination, have been used to demarcate the boundary of trespass and nuisance:
    - **(1)** Whether the defendant's action giving rise to the intrusion was committed on the plaintiff's land or outside the plaintiff's land.
    - **(2)** Whether the harm to the plaintiff's land was direct or indirect.
    - **(3)** Whether the invasion was committed by tangible matter or some intangible substance.
    - **(4)** Whether the intrusion deprives the plaintiff of possession of the land or merely of use and enjoyment of the land.
    - In some jurisdictions, situations that would traditionally be treated as very serious nuisances can be charged as a basis for an action in trespass.
  - **Note 2**: Nuisance has a shorter statute of limitations than trespass – this may be impetus for the "modern view of trespass" which the *Adams* court decried (modern view may be motivated by sympathy for particular plaintiffs barred by shorter statute of limitations for nuisance).
  - **Note 5**: Getting a court to recognize a **purely aesthetic** nuisance is very difficult.
- *Campbell v. Seaman:* Plaintiff landowners sued defendant brickworks for nuisance after emissions from the brickworks killed the plaintiffs' trees.
  - **Holding:** Court granted plaintiffs an injunction.
  - **Rationale:**
    - **(1)** People are bound to make a reasonable use of their property so as to occasion no unnecessary damage or annoyance to their neighbors.
      - "**Reasonable use**" depends on the circumstances of the locality. To constitute a nuisance, use must be such as to produce a tangible and appreciable injury to neighboring property, or such as to render its enjoyment uncomfortable or inconvenient.
    - **(2)** Damages were irreparable – **trees and vines were unique goods.**
    - **(3)** No defense of **"coming to the nuisance"** – no proof that the plaintiffs knew that the defendant was going to use the land for a brickworks.
      - Cannot erect a nuisance upon land adjoining vacant lands owned by another, and thus control the use to which the neighbor's land could be subjected to in the future.
      - Defendant could not require a prescriptive easement to emit noxious fumes because **no continuous use of land as a brickyard for SOL of 20 years.**

- - - **(4)** Damage to plaintiff was high, damage to plaintiff was low (injunction would not destroy defendant's business because brickmaking could be done in a lot of other places).
      - If reverse had been true, then injunction might not have been granted.
    - **Note 1:** Under the locality rule, short of physical damage, if a location is particularly suited to an intense use, courts are more forgiving in the face of claims of nuisance.
- **BALACING TEST:** Trend has been towards some form of balancing. <u>First Restatement of Torts subsumed locality rule into general utilitarian balancing test.</u>
    - Test balances the gravity of harm to the plaintiffs against the social value of the activity.
      - Gravity of harm factors include:
        - **(1)** Extent and character of harm.
        - **(2)** Suitability of use to location
        - **(3)** Social value of use invaded.
      - Utility of conduct factors include:
        - **(1)** Social value of defendant's conduct.
        - **(2)** Suitability to location.
        - **(3)** Impracticability of preventing invasion.
- **Note 6:** Flat rule allowing coming to the nuisance as a defense <u>incentivizes wasteful racing behavior</u> – someone can acquire rights against neighbors simply by being first.
- **Note 7:** IN some states, one can acquire a proscriptive easement to commit a nuisance by committing the nuisance for the statutory period by prescription.
- **Note 8:** Courts are not willing to let sensitive use (e.g. residential) preclude the entrance of more intense commercial uses for all time.
- *Boomer v. Atlantic Cement Co.*: Plaintiff sought an injunction against defendant cement company.
    - **Holding:** Court denied an injunction, and instead granted permanent damages to the plaintiffs, under a "servitude on land" theory of damages.
    - **Rationale for Holding:** Large disparity in economic consequences of the nuisance and the injunction.
      - <u>Court essentially performed a balancing test.</u> – damage to landowners was relatively small, damage to cement company (and by extension jobs in the Hudson Valley) was very high.
      - Court rejected idea of granting injunction but postponing to give opportunity for technical advances because rate of research was beyond the control of the defendant (defendant was one player in a whole industry).
    - **Note 1:** Automatic injunction rule is overstated – injunctions were never completely automatic.
- *Spur Industries v. Del Webb*: Plaintiff appealed judgment that permanently enjoined it from operating a cattle feedlot near the plaintiff.
    - **Holding:** Court held that Del Webb had to indemnify Spur for a reasonable amount of the cost of relocating or shutting down its cattle feedlot.

- Court distinctly limited this relief to a case when a developer has brought into a previously agricultural or industrial area the population which made the injunction necessary (and for which the business has no adequate relief).
    - Spur was brought as a **public nuisance** action under a statute which stated that odor and flies were nuisances *per se*.
        - Public nuisance is one in which the rights enjoyed by citizens as part of the public are affected. To constitute a public nuisance, the nuisance must affect a considerable number of people or an entire community or neighborhood.
    - **Coming to the nuisance:** Courts in AZ had held that the residential landowner may not have relief if he knowingly came into a neighborhood reserved for industry or agriculture.
    - **Note 1:** Generally, something could only be a public nuisance if it was independently chargeable as a criminal offense. Gov't officials always have standing to bring a public nuisance action. Private individuals can only bring a public nuisance action if they can show that they have suffered "special injury" above and beyond that experienced by other members of the public.

CALABRESI-MELAMED SQUARE

		Mode of Protection	
		Property Rule	Liability Rule
Assignment of Entitlement	Plaintiff	**RULE 1** Plaintiff can insist on an injunction, forcing the defendant to abate the activity, or stop the nuisance-generating activity if this is not possible (*Campbell*).	**RULE 2** Defendant can take plaintiff's entitlement w/o P's consent, typically upon payment of damages (usually diminished market value of land subject to nuisance) (*Boomer v. Atlantic Cement*)
	Defendant	**RULE 3** Offensive activity can continue, and the plaintiff can get it abated or removed only by getting the **Defendant's consent.** (*Hinman*, arguably; *Tucker*).	**RULE 4** Plaintiff can force the defendant to transfer the entitlement to the plaintiff in return for a payment of monetary compensation. (*Spur v. Del Webb*)

ADVANTAGES OF PROPERTY RULES
- Court doesn't need to value damages.
- Protect winning owner's autonomy more than monetary value.
- Parties can bargain to more optimal outcome (if transaction costs are low).
- Spurs the enjoined party to innovate to abate (*Boomer*)
- Courts can realize distributional preferences.

- If transaction costs are low, courts can give party it prefers an injunction on distributional grounds and let the other party buy out the party holding the right to enjoin.

DISADVANTAGES OF PROPERTY RULES
- Suboptimal outcome if court awards property rule to lower-value user, and transaction costs are high.
- Endowment effect may impede efficient transfers over time.
- Courts may bend substantive law on liability in response to harshness of property rules (e.g. less inclined to find nuisances if injunctions are automatic?)

ECONOMIC ANALYSIS OF WHEN TO CHOOSE PROPERTY OVER LIABILITY RULES
- **If transaction costs are low: property rules.**
    - Parties can reallocate.
    - Can pursue distributional preferences, by granting property right to the party preferred on distributional grounds.
- **If transaction costs are high and the court has good info about P's harm and D's prevention costs:**
    - Conventional wisdom – damages.
        - Because parties cannot easily reallocate and court can value P's harm and D's prevention costs.
    - However, maybe the court should award the property rule to the optimal user?
        - Because the court can compare (because it has good info) about P's harm and D's prevention costs.
        - If victim's harm > D's prevention costs, Victim gets property rule.
        - If D's prevention costs > victim's harm, then D gets property rule.
- **If transaction costs are high and court lacks good info about P's harm OR D's prevention costs:**
    - Court should award **damages**, using the info it has.
    - Can't award property rules because don't know whether P's harm or D's prevention costs greater.
    - Give P damages (rule 2) if info about P's harm.
    - Give D damages (rule 4) if info about D's prevention costs.
        - P will pay D damages (if P's harm greater than D's prevention costs) or P will abate (if D's prevention costs greater than P's harm).
- **If transaction costs are high and court lacks good info about P's harm and D's prevention costs:**
    - Hard to know what to do here.
    - Might be very common that transaction costs are high and the court lacks info.
    - Remember that it is hard to know when transaction costs are high and low – they could be high if there is just 1 P and 1 D (bilateral monopoly).

NUISANCE VS REGULATION

- Why are land use and environmental regulation superior to nuisance to deal with some competing uses (Boomer majority)?
    - Individuals may have difficulty attributing their harms to an entity that they can sue
    - Victims face collective action problems organizing to sue for nuisance (but is it easier to get zoning or regulation changed?)
    - Legislatures have greater expertise, fact-finding ability
    - Cts poorly situated, lack democratic legitimacy to make necessary cost-benefit determinations (but agencies and legislatures may be captured, inertia)
    - Nuisance regulates ex post while legislatures/agencies can regulate ex ante
- Although they may be substitutes, nuisance and land use & environmental regulation are also complements

B. SERVITUDES
- Generic name for **contracts that bind successors in ownership.**
- Two principal kinds of servitudes – **easements** and **covenants**.
    - **Easement:** Functionally like a contract in which an owner agrees to waive his or her right to exclude certain kinds of intrusions by another, and give the other a right to use.
    - **Covenant:** A contract in which an owner agrees to abide by certain restrictions on the use of his or her land for the benefit of one or more others.
    - **Covenants are more of a governance mechanism; more often than easements prescribe affirmative behavior on the part of the burdened landowner.**
- Appurtenant easements always run with the land; covenants sometimes rum with the land if certain conditions are met.
- Easements have always been considered a kind of property right; covenants are usually spoken of as "promises respecting the use of land."
- **Easements have an in rem effect; covenants are more accurately thought of to be in personam.**

EASEMENTS
- Conveys the right to a particular **use of land, NOT a right to possession of land.**
- An easement differs from a mere license – a license is a waiver of the right to exclude that usually arises by contract, and is (ordinarily) regarded as being revocable.
    - By contrast, **an easement is an irrevocable conveyance of the right to engage in a particular use of the land**.
- Also differs in that an easement is not a possessory interest in land (fee, lease) – there is only a right of use.
- Why regard easements as property?
    - **(1)** Purely formal – they are created by grant rather than by contract.
    - **(2)** The feature of irrevocability – easements have a more "vested" quality that distinguishes them from gratuitous licenses and most licenses arising by contract.
    - **(3)** Easements have in rem features. **A valid easement gives rise to a general duty on the part of "all the world" not to interfere with the easement.**

- Easements Appurtenant v. Easements in Gross v. Profit a Prendre:
  - **Easement Appurtenant:** One that belongs to another parcel of land ("estate")
    - **Dominant estate/tenement:** The estate that holds and is benefited by the easement. Has the right to another's property beyond the usual bundle of rights.
    - **Servient estate/tenement:** the estate that is burdened by the easement.
    - **Example:** If Blackacre is the dominant estate, and Whiteacre the servient estate, then whomever owns Blackacre has the right to use the easement, and whomever owns Whiteacre has to allow Blackacre to use the easement.
  - **Easement in Gross:** One that belongs to a particular grantee, as opposed to a particular tract of land.
    - In England, at attempt to create an easement in gross only created a license personal to the grantee. <u>Such a conveyance was not inheritable.</u>
    - American courts have been more sympathetic to easements in gross.
      - **Reason:** The emergence of the railroad industry in 19th century America. Owners were willing to grant easements to railroads, but were more reluctant to grant fees simple in a strip of land to the railroad.
      - In America, <u>if the easement in gross is of a commercial character, it is inheritable and transferable.</u>
      - Easements in gross for purely recreational purposes are **NOT** inheritable or transferable.
    - **Example:** If Allison grants Barry (who owns Blackacre) an easement in gross, and Barry sells Blackacre to Charles, then Charles does not have access to the easement granted to Barry. Charles has to negotiate his own easement in gross.
  - **Profit a prendre ("profit"):** The right to enter onto another's land in order **to extract something of value**, such as timber, fruit from trees or fish or game from a lake or forest. It is also used to permit the extraction of surface minerals (e.g. sand and gravel).
    - Generally governed by the same rules as easements appurtenant. Grant of a profit carries an implied license to enter the land; <u>this license is irrevocable as long as the profit continues to last.</u>
- Affirmative Easements v. Negative Easements
  - **Affirmative easements:** Permit the easement holder to perform some affirmative act on the land of another (e.g. use a path, fish, cut trees).
    - Can think of an affirmative easement as permitting action on the servient tract that would otherwise be a trespass or an invasive nuisance.
    - <u>Virtually all easements are affirmative easements.</u>
  - **Negative easement:** Permits the easement holder to demand that the owner of the servient tract desist from certain actions that harm the easement holder.
    - At English common law, **only four types of negative easements:**
      - (1) Blocking sunlight from falling on windows of the dominant tenement.

- **(2)** Interfering with the flow of air in a defined channel to the dominant tenant.
- **(3)** Removing lateral support to a building on the dominant tenement.
- **(4)** Interfering with the flow of water in an artificial stream to the dominant tenement.
    - English law also permitted easements to be established by prescription in these four narrow areas.
    - American courts have been somewhat more adventuresome about permitting express negative easements outside the traditional four categories.
    - In practice, when someone wants to impose a negative duty on a servient landowner to desist from taking action that might harm the dominant tract, **this will be accomplished using covenants that run with the land**.
- Public v. Private Easements
    - **Private easement:** Authorizes specific named parties to use land for designated purposes.
    - **Public easement:** Authorizes the general public to use land for designated purposes.
        - Public access rights for recreational purposes are more likely to be held as public easements.
        - Sometimes the public holds negative easements.
- Note 2: Easements can ordinarily be subdivided.
    - **For example:** If Blackare has an easement of way over Whiteacre, and Blackacre is subdivided into four lots, **absent previous agreement to the contrary, each of the new lot owners will have an easement over Whiteacre.**

CREATION OF EASEMENTS

- Because an easement is an interest in land, **Statute of Frauds requires that easement be in writing.**
- Easements can be created **expressly** or **by law**.
- **Express easements:** Owner creates easement by giving right to use land to another party. Easement states what use is permitted, and where.
    - Easement could be created by grant, of the direct A-to-B variety.
    - Alternatively, easement could be granted by reservation to the grantor. For example, A could grant Blackacre to B, but reserve to himself an easement over Blackacre, perhaps to access other land.
    - **At common law, one could not create a grant by reservation in a third party.**
        - For example, if A granted Blackacre to B, A could not in the deed to B reserve an easement in Blackacre running to C.
        - Some modern American courts disapprove of this rule.
            - **Rationale:** This rule was designed to prevent easements from being used to get around the rules of seisin important to the feudal system. Feudalism being dead, the rule against creating easements in third parties should also be rejected.
- **Easements created by law:** Four main kinds of easements created by law.

- Easement by Implication (implied by prior use) (*Schwab* refused). The requirements are:
    - **(1)** Dominant tenement (DT) and Servient tenement (ST) were under common ownership.
    - **(2)** One parcel (DT) got benefit/advantage from other parcel (ST) before parcels were separated.
    - **(3)** This use was apparent and continuous at time of severance (shows that the use was meant to be permanent).
    - **(4)** Continuation of use is **reasonably necessary** for enjoyment of dominant estate, based on circumstances at time of severance.
- Easement by Necessity (*Schwab* refused):
    - **(1)** DT and ST were under common ownership.
    - **(2)** Common Owner (O) severs the parcel and creates a **landlocked parcel without access to public road** [parcel must be landlocked at the time of severance – cannot become landlocked later]
    - **(3)** Easement must be necessary for DT to get to public road.
        - Necessity is strictly interpreted; higher degree than reasonable necessity for prior use.
        - Necessity evaluated based on circumstances at time of severance.
    - No prior use required. The easement by necessity disappears when the necessity does (automatically in most jurisdictions).
- Prescriptive Easement (*Holbrook* refused, *Warsaw* recognized):
    - Requirements (*Holbrook*):
        - **(1)** Open use.
        - **(2)** Peaceable use.
        - **(3)** Continuous use (SOL = 15 years here).
        - **(4)** Use under a claim of right adverse to the owner.
        - **(5)** Without O's knowledge and acquiescence (O didn't assert right to exclude OR reasonable O would know OR O must have known).
    - Requirements (*Warsaw*)
        - **(1)** Open and notorious.
        - **(2)** Continuous for an uninterrupted period of SOL (5 years here).
        - **(3)** Adverse (hostile, without permission of True Owner).
        - **No need for exclusive possession (different from adverse possession).**
- Easement by Estoppel (recognized in *Holbrook*):
    - **(1)** True Owner gave permission (or at the very least acquiesced).
        - Some type of action needed by servient owner communicating permission for continued access.
    - **(2)** User relied to his detriment on the permission, by changing his position materially.
    - **(3)** Inequitable to revoke the permission.

- ***Schwab v. Timmons:*** Petitioners requested an easement by necessity or by implication for ingress, egress, and utilities over the properties owned by the respondents in order to gain access to their landlocked parcels.
    - Parcels were not landlocked at the time of conveyance; Schwabs created their landlocked parcels when they conveyed away their highway access.
    - Petitioners claimed that only access to a public road was over land to which they did not have a right-of-way (parcel was bordered by Lake Michigan to the west and a bluff on the west.
    - **Holding:** Petitioners failed to establish a claim for either an easement by implication or an easement by necessity.
        - **Easement by implication:** The private road that the petitioners sought to extend did not and never did extend to the petitioners' properties, and failed to allege that any use by the US Gov't was so obvious, manifest, or continuous as to show that it was meant to be permanent.
        - **Easement by necessity:** Failed because petitioners' parcels were not landlocked when the US (the former common owner of the parcels + one other parcel containing private road) conveyed the other parcel.
            - At the time of conveyance, the eastern boundary of the lots was east of the current boundary line.
            - Party may only avail himself of an easement by necessity when the common owner <u>severs a landlocked portion</u> of the property, and the owner of the landlocked portion cannot access a public roadway.
            - Geographical barriers (here, bluffs) **<u>do not warrant easements by necessity.</u>**
                - Grantor is not landlocked when he has difficulty getting from his land to a public road as long as he can get from his land to a public road.
    - **Note 3:** Principal reason cited by the court for the hostility towards claims of easements by implication and by necessity is that this would sanction "hidden easements" – easements that could not be discovered by searching the public records.
    - **Note 5:** About half of the states have adopted statutes that provide for condemnation of private easements for access to landlocked or inaccessible property.
        - Under these statutes, the landlocked owner can force the servient owners to convey an easement, **<u>but must pay just compensation (fair market value) for the rights so obtained</u>**.
- ***Holbrook v. Taylor*** (Kentucky 1976)*:* Appellants sought the use of a roadway over the land of another. Claimed right to the use of the roadway was by prescription or by estoppel.
    - **Holding:** No prescriptive easement, but recognized easement in estoppel.
        - **Prescriptive Easement:** No evidence that the use of the road during the period of time was adverse, continuous, or uninterrupted, thus no prescriptive easement.
        - **Easement by estoppel:** Granted. Roadway had been used since 1944 by permission of the owners of the servient estate.

- Use of the roadway to get to their home from the public highway, the use of the roadway to take in heavy equipment, material, and supplies for the construction of the residence, the general improvement of the premises, maintenance of the roadway, and the construction by appellees of a residence, all with the actual consent of the appellants or at least their tacit approval, demonstrated reliance.
- ***Warsaw v. Chicago Metallic Ceilings, Inc.*** (Cal. 1984): Plaintiff sought a prescriptive easement.
    - **Holding:** Prescriptive easement granted. Defendant not entitled to offsetting monetary relief.
    - No easement by implication b/c the possibility of creating an easement was explicitly rejected in the sale negotiations.
    - No easement by necessity b/c the plaintiffs had a driveway leading to a public road on their property (issue was that their trucks were too large to use it).
    - **Existence of prescriptive easement must be shown by a definite and certain line of travel for the statutory period.**
        - Slight deviations from the accustomed course would not defeat an easement, but substantial changes that break the continuity of the course of travel would destroy the claim to prescriptive rights.
        - Degree to which a pathway can be modified w/o destroying the easement depends on **the character of the land over which it passes, + value, improvements, and purposes to which the land is adapted.**
    - When prescriptive easement is granted, **owner of ST is not entitled to offsetting monetary relief.**
        - Court noted that it was "at least arguable" that a court of equity could order that the plaintiff contribute a portion of the cost of relocating an **innocent** encroachment as a condition of an injunction. This was not the case here however – encroachment was not innocent.
    - **Rationale for awarding easement:** Protects the reliance interest of the user.
    - **Dissent:** On the basis that the easement should be compensated the fair market value of the easement
    - **Note 2:** The standard rules of prescription and adverse possession involve Calabresian property rules.
        - One day before the SOL runs, the true owner has a property rule (can block disseisor/adverse user from further using the property without the true owner's consent.
        - One day after the SOL runs, the adverse possessor has a property rule, and can block the true owner from interfering with the use right.
        - Innovation endorsed by the California Court of Appeal would mean that the passage of the SOL would transform an entitlement in the TO protected by a property rule into an entitlement in the TO protected by a liability rule.
            - Adverse user/adverse possessor can force a transfer of use rights or possessory rights by the TO, but only upon payment of just compensation to TO.

- *Fontainebleau Hotel Corp. v. Forty-Five Twenty-Give, Inc.*: Appellees (Eden Roc Hotel) sought to enjoin the construction of an addition to the Fontainebleau that would have blocked the light and air on the Eden Roc's beach. Eden Roc also claimed that the addition was motivated by ill will and spite.
    - **Holding:** Injunction not granted.
    - **Analysis:** Court held that the maxim *sic utere tuo ut alienum non laedas* did not mean that one must **never** use his own property in such a way as to do any injury to his neighbor.
        - **Instead**, it means that one must use his property so as not to injure the lawful **rights** of another.
        - In the USA, landowner does not have a legal right to the free flow of light and air across the adjoining land of his neighbor (absent a contractual or statutory obligation).
            - Doctrine of **ancient lights** has been **unanimously repudiated** in the USA.
            - In England, landowner had no legal right in the absence of an easement or uninterrupted use and enjoyment of light for a period of 20 years.
        - **When a structure serves a useful and beneficial purpose, it does not give rise to a cause of action** either for damages or in equity.
    - **Note 3:** Most common way of providing for something like the flow of sunlight across land (other than through zoning ordinances) would be through negotiation of a restrictive covenant that limits the height of the neighboring building.
        - **Cannot obtain a restrictive covenant by prescription**.
    - **Note 7:** If structure serves no useful purpose (e.g. spite fence), then can be enjoined as a nuisance.

MISUSE OF EASEMENTS
- *Penn Bowling Recreation Center v. Hot Shoppes, Inc.*: Appellee argued that Penn Bowling had forfeited and extinguished the easement by abandonment because it had subjected appellee to an additional and enlarged use of servitude in connection with other premises to which the easement was not appurtenant.
    - **Holding:** Judgment set aside, right to apply for temporary injunction granted to appellee.
    - **Analysis.** Court made the following notes on the misuse of easements:
        - **(1)** Owner of a dominant tenement may not subject the servient tenement to use or servitude in connection with other premises to which the easement is not appurtenant.
        - **(2)** Misuse of an easement **is not sufficient to constitute a forfeiture, waiver, or abandonment of the right**.
            - Right to an easement is not lose by using it in an unauthorized manner or to an unauthorized extent **unless it is impossible to sever the increased burden so as to preserve to the owner of the DT that to**

which he is entitled and impose on the ST only the burden originally imposed upon it.
- **(3)** Authorized use and unauthorized use may be intermingled in such a way as to justify enjoining any use until the circumstances have so changed that the authorized use may be permitted w/o affording opportunity for the unauthorized use.
  - Injunction can be granted in such a case.
- **(4)** DT is entitled to a reasonable use and enjoyment of an easement – determining what a "reasonable use" is requires examining the situation of the property and the surrounding circumstances.

COVENANTS
- **Definition:** Promises to respect the use of land.
- <u>Easements</u> are fundamentally about the right to <u>go onto land</u> – they are abrogations of the servient owner's right to exclude.
- <u>Covenants</u> are generally about <u>the right to insist on the use or nonuse of land:</u> As such, they typically prescribe a more or less elaborate system of governance rules.
- <u>Easements are nearly always affirmative, covenants can be either affirmative or negative.</u>
- Two theories for allowing promises respecting the use of land to run with the land:
  - (1): Asks whether the promise is enforceable against successors as an "<u>equitable servitude</u>".
  - (2): Asks whether the promise is enforceable against successors as a "<u>real covenant</u>."
  - Often, the critical factor in determining which theory applies is the nature of the relief that the plaintiff seeks. If an <u>injunction</u> is sought, then the matter lies in equity and <u>courts will generally apply the equitable servitude theory</u>.
  - If <u>damages</u> are sought, then <u>courts will generally apply the real covenant theory.</u>
    - <u>Equitable servitudes and real covenants are the same thing</u> – promises respecting the use of land.
      - Label that attaches in deciding whether these promises run with the land is determined by the theory for enforcing the promise against successors, not by any thing intrinsic in the nature of the promise itself.
- Covenants are less "property-like" than easements, and lie closer to the contract end of the property-contract spectrum. Thus, it appears that covenants impose no duties of forbearance on third parties.

EQUITABLE SERVITUDES - BACKGROUND
- *Tulk v. Moxhay* (England 1848): Plaintiff had sold Leicester Square to one other person (it passed to defendant through mesne conveyances), with the covenant that the defendant maintain Leicester Square as an open space with a garden and pleasure ground.
  - Defendant maintained an intention to alter the character of the square garden, and asserted a right to build upon it. Plaintiff sought an injunction.
  - **Holding:** Court of Chancery enforced the covenant attached to the land, even though this was not a landlord-tenant situation (only way to get covenant run at common law).

REAL COVENANT THEORY (ACTION IN LAW – You Get Damages)

- Major issue with covenants is whether the benefits and burdens of the deal between the original parties will extend to successors of those parties – whether the benefits and burdens "**run with the land**".
- **Burden** is on the party that wishes to do something but is blocked by the covenant; **benefit** is on the party that wishes to prevent that thing from being done (seeking to enforce the covenant).
- **Covenant has to be in writing.**
- **At law**, for the **burden** of a promise to run, need to establish:
    - (1) **Intent for the burden to run:** This can be by language or inferable from the context.
        - **Example:** If A covenants to B, who has a peanut allergy, that A will not eat peanuts in the backyard, the benefit probably wouldn't run to B's successor unless the context indicates otherwise.
    - (2) **Horizontal Privity:** Original parties (covenantor and covenantee) must be in certain relationship. There are **four approaches (from strictest to least strict):**
        - **English Common Law:** Landlord-tenant relationship required (covenant in lease).
        - **Simultaneous interest** in land required (Massachusetts Rule):
            - Parties must hold simultaneous interest in the same parcel of land; e.g. L-T relationship (tenant has present estate, L has reversion); A has FSA and B has easement on the property.
        - **Successive Interest** in land required (majority view of horizontal privity):
            - Covenant made in connection with transfer of some interest in land between covenantor and covenantee **in addition to covenant itself**.
            - Grantor-grantee: O conveys Blackacre to A, prohibits A from using it for factory.
            - This formality can be overcome by using a straw transfer (A &B transfer to C, who transfers back to A&B)
        - **Third Restatement:** No horizontal privity required.
            - Third Restatement has **not** been widely adopted.
    - (3) **Vertical Privity:** Successor in interest to original covenantor must **hold an estate of equal duration** as held by the covenantor at time of covenant.
        - **Example:** No vertical privity if B owns in FSA and conveys life estate to D).
        - In L-T situations, vertical privity would be present in assignments (where they are determined by whether the whole interest is transferred), but **not in a sublease.**
        - There **is** vertical privity if B owns a FSA and conveys a fee simple determinable to D (since a FSD could theoretically be of infinite duration).
        - Successor **does not** have to own entire area of land held by original covenantor.
    - (4) **Touch and Concern:** The covenant must touch and concern the land, as discussed above. It has to relate to the land in some way.

- **This approach is abandoned in the new Restatement as well**, but no court has followed this proposed approach.
  - (5) <u>Notice:</u> This is not included in the textbook, but it is likely a requirement to enforce the burden at Common Law today, although not originally. **Notice is as defined below**.
- At law, for the **benefit** of a promise to run, there are fewer requirements, presumably because a selling landowner would have an incentive to advertise benefits, as opposed to burdens:
  - (1) <u>Intent for the benefit to run</u>
  - (2) <u>Vertical privity:</u> For the benefit to run, the successor need only succeed **to some estate, not necessarily an estate of the same duration as the covenantor's** (so this is a less stringent requirement than in the case of the vertical privity required for the burden to run).
    - No vertical privity if the successor is an adverse possessor.
  - (3) <u>Touch and concern</u>

EQUITABLE SERVITUDE THEORY (ACTION IN EQUITY – You Get Injunction/Spec. Performance)
- **At equity**, courts have been more accommodating in granting enforcement. Equity was more hospitable to affirmative covenants than was the common law. By allowing equitable enforcement of negative covenants, parties were able to expand somewhat upon the limited menu of NEGATIVE easements.
- For the **BURDEN** of a promise to run **at equity**, there must be:
  - (1) <u>Intent</u>
  - (2) <u>Notice:</u> This is characteristic of equity. **If the covenant is in the deed given to the grantee,** there is no problem enforcing it against the grantee. **If the covenant is NOT in the deed,** then actual or inquiry notice must be present.
    - **Deed notice:** Covenant is in the deed.
    - **Actual notice:** The successor is told of the covenant even though it is not in the deed.
    - **Inquiry notice** is furnished by facts that would make a reasonable person inquire further and find the covenant. This is basically constructive notice – we are saying that there are some facts which would have made a reasonable person inquire and look for a covenant.
    - <u>With the advent of recording acts, constructive notice</u> through filing in the land records is another avenue for satisfying the notice requirement.
  - (3) <u>Touch and Concern</u>
- For the **BENEFIT** of a promise to run at equity, there must be:
  - (1) <u>Intent</u>
  - (2) <u>Touch and Concern</u>

THE THIRD RESTATEMENT
- Under Third Restatement, no need for horizontal privity or for touch and concern. **By and large, it takes a more contractarian approach to servitudes**.

- In place of the traditional requirements for enforcing servitudes against successors that made the running of a servitude exceptional, the *Restatement* makes enforceability the default.
    - **Broadly speaking, this would give servitudes a strongly contractarian flavor.**
- Like the law of contracts, the Restatement features writing requirements and exceptions for violations of public policy, unconscionability, and the like.
- **Motivation for this approach:** Reflects the basic position that servitudes are useful decides that people ought to be able to use w/o artificial constraints. **The primary function of the law is to ascertain and give effect to the intent of the parties, not to force them into arbitrary transactional forms.**

- *Sanborn v. McLean*: Defendants sought to build a gas station on their land in a subdivision. Defendants were enjoined by their neighbors, who claimed that defendants' lot was subject to a covenant barring all nonresidential development.
    - Defendant insisted that there were no restrictions in their chain of title (indeed, no restrictions in deeds of 48 of 91 lots sold).
    - Could not bring a suit under real covenant theory because covenant was not written.
    - **Holding:** Injunction upheld – **common plan doctrine** meant that defendants should have realized that their land was meant to be burdened by covenant. Defendants were on inquiry notice.
        - Defendants knew that there was a subdivider, and that neighbors had all built residences. This was enough to put defendants on constructive notice.
    - **Common Plan Doctrine.** Three requirements for covenants to pass under this doctrine:
        - **(1)** There was an original common owner with a general plan (disputable here).
        - **(2)** Lot in question was intended to be restricted as part of that common plan.
        - **(3)** The person whose lot is going to be restricted **has to have been on notice of the restriction.**
        - **This doctrine is effectively meant to serve as a gap-filler.**
    - In practice today, covenants will be included in a master declaration which the deeds reference, rather than separately in individual deeds.
    - **Rationale for holding (common plan doctrine):** Protects the reliance interest of the neighbors who thought that they were purchasing properties with residential-only restrictive covenant.
        - **Counter** – Unsettles the property rights of people like the defendants who do not have the restriction in their deed.
    - "Reciprocal Negative Easement theory" – another name for the common plan doctrine.

TERMINATION OF COVENANTS

- *Bolotin v. Rindge:* Plaintiff, the owner of a lot subject to a residential-only covenant, was suing to quiet title, for the purpose of allowing him to build a commercial office building.
    - **Holding:** Judgment of trial court that declared restrictions to be unenforceable in part were reversed.

- o Changed circumstances/conditions doctrine (Bolotin formulation): A court will declare a deed restriction to be unenforceable when:
    - (1) By **reason of changed conditions;**
    - (2) Enforcement of the restrictions would be inequitable and oppressive, **and**
    - (3) Would harass plaintiff without benefiting the adjoining owners.
- o Changed circumstances test (Prof. Wyman's in-class formulation): Three elements are
    - **(1) Drastically changed conditions.**
    - **(2) In the neighborhood affected by the covenants.**
        - Problem: Defining the size of the neighborhood.
    - **(3) No longer of substantial benefit to the dominant estates.**
        - Both economic and noneconomic benefits are to be considered.
- o **Analysis:** Court's analysis concluded that there was no evidence that the purpose of the restrictions had become obsolete, or that the enforcement of the restrictions would no longer benefit the defendants.
    - Purpose of deed restriction was to preserve the tract as a residential area by excluding commercial activities, which would bring noise, traffic, congestion, and other conditions which would lessen the comfort and enjoyment of the residents.
    - Plaintiff did not cite any cases in which deed restrictions had been held unenforceable upon findings which were limited to the economic consequences.
    - The court here is basically saying that **for the doctrine to apply, the plaintiff has to pass the Pareto test for efficiency.**

C. Public Regulations of Land Use
ZONING AND OTHER LAND USE REGULATION

- Main source of land use control of a public character today is zoning and related land-use regulation.
- Zoning arose in the early 20th century as a response to inadequacies of nuisance and covenants to secure a stable regime of residential land use in an urban society.
- **Definition of zoning:** Regulation of land use through a general regime permitting and forbidding particular uses of land in certain locations.
- **Earliest zoning often targeted the characteristics of the user, and was used to enforce racial and economic segregation.**
- Zoning ordinances are a matter of state and local law. The authority to engage in zoning must come from the state. States can delegate the police power in the area of zoning to local governments. **Only the state can pass a zoning enabling act.**
- **Variances:** Allow for relaxation of zoning requirements in cases of undue hardship.
- **Special exemptions:** Permit uses only if conditions specified in the ordinance are met.
    - o If one satisfies criteria set out in the zoning ordinance, one has a right to a special exemption. **Variances have to be granted by the zoning board.**
- Violation of zoning ordinances are theoretically liable for civil and criminal sanctions, although enforcement is sometimes spotty.

- In courts, **Board of Zoning Appeals is treated like a quasi-judicial administrative agency** – principles of due process and administrative law apply.
- *Village of Euclid v. Ambler Realty Co.:* The case which effectively legalized modern zoning nationally.
    - **The Zoning Scheme:** Six classes of use districts (inclusive); Three classes of height districts (inclusive); four classes of area districts (inclusive)
        - Appellant's tract of land came under mostly residential zones (no industry, very few commercial activities allowed).
    - **Grounds for attack on zoning ordinance:** (1) ordinance was in derogation of the 14th Amendment in that it deprived defendant of liberty and property without due process of law, (2) it violated certain provisions of the Ohio Constitution.
        - **Remedy sought:** An injunction restraining the enforcement of the ordinance.
    - **Bottom-line holding:** Zoning ordinances are **not** presumptively unconstitutional, and can only be struck down if they are **clearly arbitrary and unreasonable, having no substantial relation to the public health, safety, morals, or general welfare.**
        - Ordinance justified as a proper exercise of the police power.
        - Question of whether the power exists to forbid certain land uses is determined by **considering the proposed land use (e.g. commercial) in connection with the circumstances and locality**.
    - When land use regulations are analyzed, especially under the Takings Clause (see below), **analogies are often drawn to nuisance.**
    - Most judicial action regarding zoning ordinances happen at the state level – state courts vary greatly in how deferential they are to local zoning authorities.
    - **Note 1:** Difference between cumulative zoning and non-cumulative zoning
        - **Cumulative zoning:** Ordinance defines a hierarchy of uses. In any zone of a given level, one can have uses of that level or any "higher" use.
        - **Noncumulative zoning:** One can only have enumerated uses in any given zone (e.g. no residential uses in a commercial zone).

NONCONFORMING USES
- Zoning ordinances typically grandfather in nonconforming uses of property in existence when a zoning scheme is enacted.
    - **For example, a commercial business in a residential area will be allowed to continue.**
- Once a use of property is established it becomes a "vested right."
    - In contrast, an owner of undeveloped land has no vested right to any particular type of use, nor does the owner of property dedicated to a particular use have a vested right to switch to a different use.
        - **These have become established points of reference in zoning law.**
- *Harbison v. City of Buffalo:* Petitioners had an existing nonconforming use in a residential zone.
    - **City's argument:** Ordinance requiring the termination of petitioners' nonconforming use of the premises as a junkyard within three years was a valid exercise of the police power. Claim **not based on the theory of nuisance.**

- Owners of property using their premises in a manner forbidden by a zoning ordinance upon its adoption **must be given a degree of protection (this is constitutionally required).**
- **Bottom-line holding:**
    - **(1)** Reasonable termination periods for prior nonconforming structures are not unconstitutional.
    - **(2)** Analogously, zoning ordinances may provide that, at the end of a period of permitted nonconformity, the nonconforming use must cease ("**Amortization**").
    - **(3)** In ascertaining the length of a reasonable period of permitted nonconformity, a **balance must be found between social harm and private injury.**
    - **(4)** To be constitutionally valid, termination provisions must be reasonable "in the light of the nature of the business of the property owner, the improvements erected on the land, the character of the neighborhood, and the detriment caused the property owner"
- **Rationale:** Policy of nonconforming uses was based upon the assumption that the ultimate end of zoning would be accomplished as the nonconforming use terminated with time. **This was not proven to be the case – many nonconforming uses flourished from the lack of competition.**
    - [Own thought]: Analogous to creating a state-supported monopoly or oligopoly in certain areas.
- **Dissent: (1)** Concerned that this would stifle economic development – businessmen might hesitate to invest in a store if they knew that their investment could be "expropriated" after a period of time if a special interest group got the zoning code changed; **(2)** Would incentivize owners of nonconforming uses to not upkeep their properties.
- Note 3 – **Uncertainty sometimes about whether amortization may be found to be a taking.**

ZONING POLICY

- Case for zoning rests on its potential to deal with land use externalities, rampant market failure and collective-action problems.
    - Covenants not an adequate response to zoning problems in established neighborhoods because **transaction costs of setting up covenants in established areas is too high for covenants to be effective.**
    - Nuisance law inadequate to control incompatible land uses because:
        - **(1)** land uses might not rise to the level of a common-law nuisance.
        - **(2)** Judges are ill-equipped to supply detailed governance regimes to prescribe proper use.
        - **(3)** Nuisance law not well-equipped to consider the externalities associated with land use (e.g. can only award damages to compensate the landowners who brought the suit – cannot award damages to offset damage to general environment).

- Zoning can play a role in the competition of localities for residents. If localities can offer different packages of taxes and public goods, residents can sort themselves into the places that most suit them (**Tiebout Hypothesis**)
    - <u>Essential to this type of competition is that those who do not pay can be excluded from the benefits.</u>
        - That is, only people who pay taxes will enjoy the schools, parks, etc. that those taxes fund.
        - For those who support this type of interjurisdictional competition, zoning is viewed as a tool to prevent "fiscal freeriding" by allowing municipalities to select the types of land use that they wish to attract or avoid.
            - Has an effect on the price of houses (and by extension municipal property tax revenues).
- Problems with comprehensive planning/zoning laws:
    - **(1)** Failures of urban renewal in the mid-20th century (emphasis on extreme separation of uses, large-scale planning – e.g. Cabrini-Green).
    - **(2)** Zoning subject to the limits of bureaucratic decisionmaking, including rigidity, high admin. costs, and blunt incentives – resulting in uniformity and lack of attention.
    - **(3)** Developers and homeowners may use the zoning process to engage in rent seeking behavior, restricting the supply of housing, and creating local monopolies.
    - **(4)** Large lot requirements can cause urban sprawl, raise housing costs, and promote class/racial segregation.

EXCLUSIONARY ZONING

- *Southern Burlington County NAACP v. Township of Mt. Laurel*: Suit alleging that defendant's land use regulations resulted in the unlawful exclusion of low and moderate income families from the township.
    - **The Facts:** Zoning ordinance in force meant that the balance of the Township's land area had been developed in the conventional form of major subdivisions.
        - General ordinance provided for four residential areas, all of which only permitted only single-family detached dwellings. **No apartments, townhouses, or mobile homes were allowed.** Result was intensive, low-density development.
        - Newly approved planned unit developments (PUDs) provided for multi-family housing, but this housing was **beyond the financial reach of low and moderate income families, esp. those with young kids.**
        - Only middle and upper income people were sought as township residents.
        - Active opposition by Twp. government with respect to affording any opportunity for decent housing for the Twp's poor residents (most of whom lived in slum housing).
    - **The Legal Issue:** Whether a developing municipality like Mount Laurel could make it physically and economically impossible to provide low and moderate income housing in the municipality.
    - **Holding:** Every municipality must, by its land use regulations, presumptively make realistically possible an appropriate variety and choice of housing.

- More specifically, cannot prevent low and moderate income people from living in the township.
- **Rationale:** Provision of adequate housing was absolutely essential to the promotion of the general welfare required in all local land use regulation.
  - **Township's rationale for exclusionary zoning:**
    - **(1)** The idea that every municipality may, by the exercise of the zoning power, allow only such uses and to such extent as will be beneficial to the local tax rate.
    - **(2)** Classism and racism.
    - **(3)** Collective action problem – municipalities individually try to avoid the affordable housing that they collectively need.
- **Benefits of reducing exclusionary zoning:**
  - **(1)** Might reduce concentrated poverty in the inner cities.
  - **(2)** May benefit poorer households, who might be able to afford suburbs.
  - **(3)** Reduces sprawl, congestion, pollution.
  - **(4)** Agglomeration benefits from denser housing that permits multiple employers to locate nearby.
- **Regional planning:** Court noted that it might make more sense to have more of some kinds of housing in one municipality in a region than in another, because of greater availability of suitable land, location of employment, accessibility of public transport, etc.
  - However, <u>NJ legislation meant that zoning could only be on an individual municipal basis, rather than regionally.</u>
    - So long as this remained the case, NJ Court felt that every municipality had to bear its fair share of the regional burden.
- **The Mount Laurel Saga:**
  - **Mount Laurel II:** All municipalities must provide their fair share of opportunity for low and moderate income housing based on regional need.
    - <u>**Builder's remedy:**</u> Allows builders to build if municipalities don't meet obligations.
  - **1985 – Fair Housing Act:** Creates Council on Affordable Housing to take the process out of courts.
    - Municipalities can sell up to 50% of their obligations to other municipalities under Regional Contribution Agreements (abolished in 2008)
  - **1986 – Mount Laurel III:** Upholds Fair Housing Act.
  - **2013 – Mount Laurel IV:** NJ Supreme Court invalidates COAH regulations determining municipal fair shares using novel "growth share" method as inconsistent with FHA.
  - **2015 – Mount Laurel V:** NJ Supreme Court holds that the admin. process is nonfunctional and returns to the courts.
  - Overall, Mount Laurel has not been very successful – over 80% of NJ's poor depend on housing made available through means other than Mount Laurel.
    - Primary beneficiaries have been white elderly women.

INCLUSIONARY ZONING
- Name given to a program by which developers (voluntarily or otherwise) set aside a certain percentage of units in newly constructed housing developments for occupation by low-income people.
- **Appeal:** <u>(1)</u> Developers pay for it, so it has no direct fiscal cost at a time when direct subsidy dollars for affordable housing are scarce; <u>(2)</u> Produces "economic integration" – high and low income households live on the same hallways.
- **Problems:** <u>(1)</u> Affordable housing is extremely expensive; <u>(2)</u> May lead to a chilling effect on the construction of new developments (fewer built because it is too costly to developers).

TAKINGS
A. Public Use
- **Takings Clause of the 5th Amendment:** "Nor shall private property be taken for public use without just compensation"
    - Applies directly to the federal government, and has been held to apply to the states through the Due Process Clause of the 14th Amendment.
- **Eminent Domain:** A tool the government can use to break bilateral monopolies/solve holdout problems when it needs to assemble land for a public project.
    - Not allowing eminent domain would require the government to negotiate with individual landowners for easements. This would be expensive and prejudicial to the taxpayers in cases involving extreme holdouts.
    - Allowing the government to confiscate land without compensation would impose disproportionate burdens on a few landowners for the benefit of the public at large, might encourage the government to engage in excessive confiscations of property, and might discourage investment in property that could be subject to uncompensated expropriations.
- Power of compulsory transfer is obviously an exception to the ordinary rules associated with property ownership.
    - Eminent domain transforms Calabresian property rule protection into liability rule protection.
- Eminent domain is a public power, and cannot be exercised by a private person unless there has been a valid delegation of eminent domain power to that person (e.g. common carriers and private utility companies).
- <u>Principal constitutional requirements are that the project be a "public use" and that the condemning authority has offered the property owner "just compensation."</u>

THE PUBLIC USE REQUIREMENT
- Eminent domain must be deployed for a "public use."
- **Restrictive View:** The idea that public use actually means "use by the public" – e.g. property could be taken for highways or parks but not for factories or private homes.
    - SCOTUS has never looked upon this view favorably.
- <u>SCOTUS has always construed the public use requirement in the 5th Amendment to mean public advantage or benefit.</u>

- o Under this broader interpretation, eminent domain can be used for any project that has some public interest rationale. SCOTUS has also said that courts should give great deference to legislative bodies in their determinations of what sorts of projects satisfy the public use requirement.
- o Federal courts have almost never invalidated a taking of property for failing the public use requirement
- **Kelo v. City of New London**: City authorized the New London Development Corporation (a city organ) to acquire property using ED. The NLDC initiated condemnation proceedings to acquire a few holdout parcels in a 90 acre tract of land that was slated to be turned over to Pfizer to build a new research facility. The City hoped that this would bring in more jobs and revitalize the local economy.
  - o **Question:** Whether a city's decision to take property for the purpose of economic development satisfies the "public use" requirement of the Fifth Amendment.
  - o **Holding:** Yes, it does.
  - o **Majority (Stevens):** Public use = public purpose.
    - Public use must not be pretext for private purpose.
  - o **Kennedy's Concurrence:** Public use = public purpose.
    - Subject to meaningful rational basis review of record that public purpose not a pretext for private benefit.
  - o **O'Connor's Dissent:** ED allows for public purpose only if government eliminating harmful use/preventing affirmative harm to society.
    - No economic development taking if not eliminating a harmful use.
    - Distinguished *Berman* (taking in the context of urban renewal) and *Midkiff* (taking to redistribute land that was concentrated in the hands of a few owners, thus creating rental market oligopoly) on the grounds that takings there were eliminating harm.
      - *Midkiff* involved the redistribution of land in the first instance to private owners (O'Connor wrote the majority opinion in that case), similarly to the redistribution in *Kelo*.
  - o **Thomas's Dissent:** ED only allowed if land will be government owned or used by the public.
    - No economic development taking.
    - Noted that takings (urban renewal programs in particular) were associated with the displacement of blacks.
  - o **Note 1:** There was a major political backlash to the *Kelo* decision – 43 states adopted new laws or ballot measures in response to the decision, most of which either severely restricted or prohibited the use of takings for economic development.
  - o **Note 5:** The Court in *Berman* and *Midkiff* noted that eminent domain was conterminous with the police power. <u>The point that the Court seemed to be making when it uttered those words was that the government could use the power of eminent domain to achieve any purpose within the permissible ends of government.</u>
    - This would seem to compel the conclusion that eminent domain can be used for economic development.

- o **Note 6:** The holdout problem is a very important justification for the power of eminent domain.

B. JUST COMPENSATION
- Other significant constitutional limitation on eminent domain is **that the condemning authority must pay "just compensation."**
- *United States v. Miller*: Case dealt with the proper standard for valuing property taken for public use.
  - o Holding:
    - **(1)** Fair market value is to be ascertained **as of the date of taking.**
      - However, courts might use the date of the start of the trial.
    - **(2)** Subjective valuation of the land by the owner is not to be taken into account.
    - **(3)** If the government takes a tract of land, and **at a later date** decides to take other lands whose value has gone up because of the first taking, **then the gov't must pay the enhanced market value.**
      - **(3a): However,** if the public project **from the beginning** included the taking of certain tracts but only one of them is taken in the first instance, then the increased value of the other lands is not to be taken into account. **The court awards compensation as of the date that the government committed to the project.**
        - o **Example:** If authorization of condemnation comes in August 1937, and the actual condemnation order comes down a year later, market value is the value of the land as of August 1937.
    - **(4)** Payment at time of condemnation is of estimated compensation – it is intended as a provisional settlement. If compensation is too high, then receiving parties have to pay back the excess.
      - **Reasons: (1)** Want to give the government immediate possession of the property, and to relieve it of the burden of accruing interest; **(2)** Give the former owner immediate cash compensation to the extent of the government's estimate of the value of the property.
- Fair Market Value is Often Undercompensatory
  - o FMV doesn't compensate for:
    - **(1)** Subjective or idiosyncratic values.
    - **(2)** Social capital or community connections.
    - **(3)** Loss of autonomy from forced sale.
    - **(4)** Assembly surplus – extra value from combining property with other property.
    - Property rules – injunctions – are better at protecting subjective value than liability rules.
    - Undercompensatory aspect of FMV helps explain the focus on public use (*Kelo*).
  - o **Note 1:** Variety of approaches for estimating fair market value –

- **(1)** Examine recent transactions in which the property was sold, and adjust for general changes in market prices in the area since the date of the transactions.
- **(2)** Examine recent transactions of other parcels of property in the area, similar to the property in question, and adjust for differences in size, location, and quality of improvements.
- **(3)** Estimate the rental value of the property in question, and capitalize this to reach a purchase price using a rate of return commonly used as a benchmark for real estate investments in the area.
- **(4)** Determine the replacement cost of the land and improvements taken, and adjust downward to reflect depreciation due to age and wear and tear.
    - **Note 2:** In economic terms, the *Miller* court above can be read as saying that the owner should be awarded the <u>opportunity cost</u> of having his land taken away. <u>Opportunity cost is the highest and best use of the land other than the use proposed by the condemning authority.</u>
    - **Note 3:** *Miller* court also concludes that just compensation means that the owner is not entitled to an award based on the after-condemnation value of property in the area.
        - **Rationale:** Do not want to confer a windfall on the condemnee – <u>condemnee has done nothing to create this enhanced value (reaping w/o sowing).</u>
        - Valuing condemned property on a post-condemnation basis would be self-defeating insofar as the public benefits of the taking would be capitalized in the land values and transferred to the condemnee.
    - **Note 4:** There is a strong efficiency argument, in the context of when the government takes a tract of land and then later decides to take more, for awarding the condemnee the current value of the land.
        - We want the government to take into account all the costs of enacting its public project, including the costs of land.
    - **Note 5**: Ordinarily, the temporal reference point for determining fair market value is the date at which title transfers. However, court departs from this reference point when determining whether respondent's property was part of a single government project.
    - **Note 6:** Another objection to the fair market value formula is that it provides no recovery for the subjective value that owners attach to their property.
    - **Note 7:** Less drastic proposal for dealing with the problem of subjective value would be to pay a bonus above fair market value, at least for certain categories of takings.
        - This system might create a risk of overcompensating property owners who do not attach must subjective value to their holdings.
    - **Note 8 – Reasons for sticking to fair market value:**
        - **(1)** Difficulty of valuing things like subjective value or consequential damages. Including such things would increase the admin. costs of eminent domain.
        - **(2)** Eminent domain will be used only for public projects that provide public goods that benefit everyone in the community. These sorts of projects arguably deserve public subsidies, and one form the subsidies can take is by

providing less than full compensation to those whose property is condemned (i.e. by not taking into account subjective valuation).
- **Note 9**: How do we determine just compensation when the government takes a **portion** of a parcel rather than the whole thing? Established rule is that the landowner is entitled to the fair market value of what is taken plus "severance damages" for any loss in value to the part that is not taken.
  - Rule for partial takings only applies when a partial taking affects a single parcel.

QUICK TAKE STATUTES

- Condemnation in *Miller* occurred pursuant to the federal version of what are called "quick take" statutes.
  - These statutes are meant to streamline eminent domain proceedings by transferring title to the condemning authority before all contested issues raised by the condemnation have been resolved.
  - In early years, title to property acquired by ED did not pass to the condemning authority until all issues, including the amount of compensation to be paid, had been resolved.
    - Resulted in long, drawn-out affairs, which increased the costs of eminent domain.
- **Quick-take statutes**: Generally provide that if the government deposits with the court the estimated value of the property, and the court is satisfied that the government has legal authority to condemn and that the project is for a public use, then the government can obtain title to the property before a final judgment fixing the amount of compensation is reached.
  - As soon as title transfers, the condemned party must move out.
  - If gov't's estimate is too low, gov't must make up the difference (with interest) once the final judgment is entered.
  - If estimate is too high, government can sue to get the money back.
  - It is settled that quick take procedures are constitutional, provided that the government deposits a fair estimate of just compensation with the court before title passes and the taking is otherwise legally justified.

C. REGULATORY TAKINGS

- Derives from the understanding that the government's power of ED is distinct from its police power.
- When the government regulates property under the police power – for example, when it adopts zoning or other regulations designed to reduce negative externalities associated with incompatible land use – then it is understood that there is no constitutional requirement that the government compensate property owners for losses they may suffer due to the regulations.
- Regulatory takings doctrine says that if the government regulates property in an especially severe way, the regulation will be deemed to be a "taking" of private property, just as if the government had exercised the power of eminent domain.

- When this happens, the government must pay the owner just compensation for the value of the property taken, just as it would if the government had instituted a formal ED proceeding.

WHY REGULATORY TAKINGS DOCTRINE?
- Anti-evasion principle
- Fairness: some people shouldn't have to bear burdens which should be borne by the public
- Cost internalization to promote efficient government decision-making
- Os won't invest if property rights insecure
- Protects politically powerless property Os
- Signals societal commitment to individual liberty

- ***Pennsylvania Coal Co. v. Mahon***: This is the case where the modern regulatory takings doctrine began to take shape.
    - Majority (Holmes) and dissent (Brandeis) considered the same three factors.
        - **(1)** No taking if the state acted within the police power.
        - **(2)** If the state is not acting within the police power, does regulation go too far or diminish property values too much?
        - **(3)** If the state is not acting within the police power, is there average reciprocity of advantage?
            - Holmes said that there was no average reciprocity of advantage because the whole burden was being imposed on the mining companies.
    - In effect, the judges are disagreeing on **the baseline for determining whether the regulation has gone too far.**
        - Holmes is saying that the baseline is the support estate, and that the numerator is also the support estate – therefore, 100% of the private property is taken.
            - In modern terms, we would say that **Holmes is engaging in conceptual severance.** This is a strategy enabled by thinking of property as a bundle of rights.
                - If the government has taken any stick from the bundle of rights, the government has taken one's property under this concept.
        - Brandeis is saying that the baseline is the support estate plus something else, and that the numerator is the support estate.
    - **Note 5:** Regulatory takings adopts a liability rule rather than a property rule for protecting property rights (using the Calabresian terms). This distinction has important procedural consequences for raising regulatory takings issues.
        - For example, it means that a claimant must exhaust possible procedures for obtaining compensation before challenging a regulation as being an unconstitutional regulatory taking.
    - **Note 7:** In considering the broad run of cases, it seems reasonably clear that it is **not** considered to be a taking for the government to impose the functional equivalent of

a servitude on parties who conceivably could have agreed to one as a matter of voluntary negotiation.
- **The "Conflagration Rule"** – blowing up a house to stop a conflagration is not regarded as a taking requiring the payment of compensation.

ACADEMIC PERSPECTIVES ON REGULATORY TAKINGS
- Broadly speaking, academic "takings" theories fall into three categories.
- **Theory 1:** One type of theory, which is doctrinal in nature, attempts to define more precisely the distinction between governmental powers, and in particular the distinction between the power of eminent domain and the police power.
    - One formulation distinguishes between actions taken by the government when acting in an "enterprise" capacity, where compensation was required, and actions taken in "mediating" between incompatible uses of property, where no compensation was required.
    - A less conceptual approach posits that courts should start with ideal typical situations governed by one power or the other, and then reason by analogy from the settled understandings in fitting novel situations into the picture.
        - For example, seizing possession of land = taking, while ordering an owner to stop polluting = police power (abatement of nuisances). Armed with these paradigmatic situations, courts should then seek to decide disputed cases by attempting to determine whether the challenged action falls closer to the eminent domain end of the spectrum or the police power end of the spectrum.
- **Theory 2:** Focuses on the impact of the government action on the property owner, and posits that the regulatory takings doctrine is designed to redress actions that have an unfair distributional impact for the owner.
    - One theory (Frank Michelman) suggests assessing takings claims using utilitarian theory and Rawlsian theories of justice.
        - Whenever "demoralization costs (the psychological pain incurred by owners and their sympathizers from government action that reduces the value of their property, plus the foregone investment) are higher than the cost of paying compensation and administering a compensation system, then the government should pay compensation.
    - Very different conception (Richard Epstein) argued that all government actions that disturb the existing distribution of wealth are constitutionally problematic.
        - Unless the government is redressing a wrong committed by an owner, compensation is required.
    - Third approach grounded in distributional concerns would limit the scope of protection to measures that "single out" a relatively small number of owners for uniquely severe burdens while providing general benefits to everyone else.
        - Measures having a general impact would not require compensation because they would be presumed to be subject to effective control by the political process.

- o One implication of these theories is that we need an overarching theory of distributive justice.
    - Note further that under these various theories it does not matter what sort of power the government is exercising in determining whether it has committed a taking.
- **Theory 3:** Third type of theory focuses on the government and how a compensation requirement might improve the functioning of the government.
    - o One theme is that compensation may improve the efficiency of government by requiring the government to "internalize" the costs its regulations impose on property owners.
        - If government can impose regulations without regard to the cost, it may suffer from the fiscal illusion that these regulations are costless, with the result that the government may engage in excessive regulation.
        - By contrast, if the government must compensate for the losses incurred by owners, the government may impose only those regulations that yield more in benefits to society than the costs imposed on owners.
    - o **Criticisms:**
        - **(1)** Cost internalization works both ways – the government should have an incentive not to impose unnecessary costs on property owners, but property owners should have an incentive not to impose unnecessary costs on everyone else.
            - Therefore, requiring the government to compensate owners for every regulation that reduces the value of the owner's property would undermine the effectiveness of government efforts to stop property owners from imposing harms on others.
        - **(2)** Government may underregulate unless it is required to compensate property owners.

            - Argument here is that property owners who do not receive compensation when the government regulates them in a way that significantly affect their property values will form a powerful lobby that can block the regulation.
            - Compensation neutralizes intense opposition to government policies that promote the general welfare.
- *Penn Central v. City of New York*: Concerned the issue of whether a historic preservation law constituted a regulatory taking.
    - o Court identified several factors of particular significance:
        - **(1)** Extent of diminution in the value of the property (denominator = property as a whole under Penn Central) – i.e. the economic impact of the regulation.
            - Follows Brandeis's formulation of the denominator in *Pennsylvania Coal Co.*

- Numerator = value of the property after the regulation (taking into account any government offsets such as transferable development rights.
        - **(2)** Interference with reasonable investment-backed expectations.
        - **(3)** Character of the government action (physical invasion or public program).
    - Court noted that the NYC law did not interfere at all with the present use of Grand Central Terminal.
    - **Dissent (Rehnquist):** Held that there was a taking on the basis that Penn Central could not build on top of the terminal without first getting the permission of the City Landmark Preservation Commission
        - City was not trying to abate a nuisance, but instead placed an **affirmative** duty on Penn Central to maintain the Terminal in its present state and in "good repair."
    - **Note 4:** Important to note that two of the factors considered key in *Mahon* – whether the regulation seeks to prevent a nuisance and whether it provides a reciprocity of advantage – disappear from the formulaic requirement.
    - **Note 6:** One way to interpret this case is that the government can abrogate an owner's right to destroy property without incurring any takings liability, at least when the financial burden is not too extreme.
    - **Note 8:** Some commentators have noted that "freezing" the exterior design of notable buildings without providing any compensation for lost development rights may have two unintended consequences.
        - **(1)** Persons who own buildings that are potential targets for historical preservation designation may rush to demolish them before they are protected.
        - **(2)** Persons who are contemplating commissioning the construction of new buildings may turn down dramatic or innovative designs out of fear that they will be "rewarded" with a historic preservation designation, and hence will be locked into the building for all time.

Themes In Justice Brennan's Rejection of Penn Central's As Applied Takings Challenge
- Regulation not a problematic **diminution in value** b/c:
    - Only a partial taking
        - denominator is parcel as a whole (1291), not the air rights
            - City tax block designated as landmark site (1291)
            - City tax block plus 8 other property to wh/ TDRs could be transferred (1293)
    - Penn Central might still be able to use some of airspace above Grand Central
    - Air rights can be transferred to other sites (using TDRs), and these TDRs have other value that counts in deciding whether there is a taking
        - Compare Rehnquist and Scalia (in Suitum): TDRs are relevant in deciding whether "just compensation" has been paid, not taking
- Penn Central's **primary expectation** is protected
    - its present use of Terminal is protected

- It can still obtain reasonable return on its investment
- As in Harbison, law is protecting present uses (reasonable investment-backed expectations)
- **Penn Central is not being singled out** according to Brennan (compare Rehnquist)
    - Burden is part of comprehensive landmark protection plan (foreshadows Kelo's emphasis on the "plan")
    - Preserving landmarks benefits all New Yorkers economically and by improving quality of life (per Brandeis in Mahon)

- *Loretto v. Teleprompter Manhattan CATV Corp.*: Question here was whether a minor but permanent physical occupation of an owner's property authorized by the government constituted a "taking" of property for which just compensation is required.
    - **Holding (Marshall):** Physical occupation of property authorized by the government is a taking, without regard to the public interest that it may serve or the size of the property taken (even *de minimis* occupation constitutes a taking).
    - Majority drew a distinction between the physical occupation of property authorized by the government and government regulations of rental units requiring landlords to comply with building codes and install smoke detectors (for example) – the latter does not involve the physical occupation of the landlord's property by a third party.
    - **Footnote 12:** Temporary limitations on the right to exclude (e.g. intermittent flooding) are subject to a more complex balancing process to determine whether they are a taking.
    - **Footnote 19:** If the statute in question here required landlords to provide cable installation if a tenant so desired, then the statute would present a different question, since the landlord would own the installation (thus it would not be a taking).
    - **Note 3:** This ruling, carving out an exception for permanent physical invasions, makes perfect sense when considering the history of eminent domain law. Historically, public utility companies would acquire easements to lay down infrastructure through the use of eminent domain. When a new public utility comes around (cable television), it seems only natural that the newcomers should also have to use eminent domain to acquire rights to run their wires from building to building.
    - **Note 4:** The combination of *Penn Central* and *Loretto* suggests that regulatory takings doctrine partakes of a general "ad hoc" test, supplemented by narrow rules of "per se" liability that apply in particular circumstances. This is similar to the approach of antitrust law, which follows a general "rule of reason" in determining whether particular restraints on trade violate the law, supplemented by per se rules that apply to conduct that seems to warrant liability without regard to the circumstances.
    - **Note 7:** After this case, the Court generally interpreted the exception for permanent occupations narrowly.
- *Lucas v. South Carolina Coastal Council:* Question of whether a statute that had a dramatic effect on the economic value of plaintiff's lots accomplished a taking of private property under the 5th and 14th Amendments, requiring just compensation.
    - **Holding:** When a regulation denies **all** economically beneficial or productive uses of land to a landowner, then there has been a taking.

- - - Compensation is required unless the law does no more than duplicate the result that could have been achieved in the courts under the law of nuisance (or the conflagration rule).
    - **Powerpoint formulation:** Restriction eliminating <u>all economically beneficial use of property</u> is a per se taking UNLESS it inheres in the <u>background principles of the State's law of property and nuisance.</u>
      - **Example:** Owner of a lakebed would not be entitled to compensation if he was denied a permit to engage in a landfilling operation that would have had the effect of flooding the land of others (since the flooding would have been a nuisance).
  - Total takings inquiry requires analysis of, among other things, the following factors:
    - <u>(1)</u> The degree of harm to public lands and resources or adjacent private property.
    - <u>(2)</u> The social value of the claimant's activities and their suitability to the location in question.
    - <u>(3)</u> The relative ease with which the alleged harm could be avoided by measures taken by the claimant and the government (or adjacent private landowners) alike.
    - The fact that a particular use has been engaged in for a long time by similarly situated owners ordinarily imports a lack of any common-law prohibition, as does the fact that other landowners, similarly situated, are permitted to continue the use denied to the claimant.
  - **Kennedy's Concurrence:** Agreed that nuisance prevention accords with the most common expectations of property owners who face regulation, but did not agree that this could be the sole source of state authority to impose severe restrictions.
  - **Blackmun's Dissent:** Argued that there was no clear and accepted "historical compact" or "understanding of our citizens" justifying the Court's new takings doctrines doctrine.
  - **Stevens's Dissent:** Argued that the Court's rule was wholly arbitrary, in that a landowner whose property was diminished in value 95% recovers nothing, while an owner whose property is diminished 100% recovers the land's full value.
- **Notes:** "Total wipeout rule" is not a clear rule for 2 reasons
  - Relies on distinction b/n total and partial takings
    - To determine if there's total or taking, need a baseline
    - Scalia punts on how to define the baseline b/c trial court determined all economic value taken
    - Gestures to using "reasonable expectations based on state law" (1318 n. 7)
    - Recall emphasis on parcel as a whole in Penn Central, Tahoe-Sierra
  - Principles of State property law & nuisance not clear
    - Nuisance not stable (muddy, state variation, politically insulated?)
    - Other background principles could include:
      - State acting in emergency to prevent spread of fire (1322, n. 16)
      - Pre-existing permanent easement (public trust)

- Statutory restrictions?
  » Palazzolo: preexisting regulations not automatic bar (1332)
- Is Lucas per se rule justified? (1318)
  - Total deprivation=physical expropriation to O
  - No reciprocity of advantage when total wipeout
  - Total wipeouts are rare
  - Total wipeouts carry risk that property pressed into public service
- Lucas hasn't had much bite in practice
  - Note 2 – We now have at least two per se rules of liability:
    - **(1)** For permanent physical occupations.
    - **(2)** For regulations that deprive owners of "all economically beneficial or productive use of land."
      - In more recent decisions, Thomas and Scalia have indicated that they understand "productive" use of land in *Lucas* to mean when the government has denied the owner the right to build on or otherwise economically extract value from the land, as by farming.
      - An alternative understanding would be that an owner is deprived of all economically beneficial or productive use of land when the land has a fair market value of zero. If this were the rule, then very few regulations would qualify.
  - Note 3: There may be other candidates for rules of per se takings liability: <u>Formal exercises of eminent domain obviously qualify</u>.
    - In *Tahoe-Sierra Preservation Council*, the Court rejected the argument that regulations that <u>temporarily</u> deprive owners of all economically beneficial use should receive per se treatment, and held instead that such regulations should be assessed under the ad hoc test of *Penn Central*.
  - Note 7: *Palazzolo v. Rhode Island*: Court held that preexisting regulations and their impacts on <u>reasonable investment-backed expectations</u> are just another factor to be considered under the *Penn Central* test.

THE DENOMINATOR PROBLEM

- The denominator problem is critical under the Lucas "total takings" test, at least if we interpret that test to mean that the regulation has deprived the owner of 100% of the value of the property.
  - Alternative interpretation is that the regulation has deprived the owner of all opportunity to engage in productive use of the land.
- For purposes of either a diminution in value analysis under *Penn Central* or the total takings test in *Lucas*, the courts must do a before and after comparison of values. <u>**More precisely, they must compare the numerator (the value of the property taken by the regulation) to the denominator (the value of the property before the regulation).**</u>
- In recent opinions, the Court has generally endorsed the idea that the denominator should be the plaintiff's "whole parcel." (Closer to Brandeis than to Holmes).

- Only hint that Scalia provides in *Lucas* about how the denominator should be identified in contested cases is that "the answer to this difficult question may lie in how the owner's reasonable expectations have been shaped by the state's law of property – i.e. whether and to what degree the state's law has accorded legal recognition and protection to the particular interest in land with respect to which the takings claimant alleges a diminution in (or elimination of) value."
- Potential issues about the proper definition of the denominator continue to arise post-*Lucas*.
  - ***Tahoe-Sierra Preservation Council*** held that a temporary moratorium on development should be assessed under the ***Penn Central*** ad hoc approach rather than the categorical approach of *Lucas*.
    - Rationale: Denominator should not be defined unduly narrowly in temporal terms any more than in physical terms.
- Major source of ambiguity concerns the exact dimensions of the "whole parcel" in any given situation.

THE MEANING OF "PROPERTY" FOR REGULATORY TAKINGS PURPOSES

- In most cases, there is no dispute about whether the interest allegedly taken is actually "property". However, we do sometimes get cases where regulatory takings claims present more novel types of interests.
- <u>SCOTUS has said that whether a claimant has "private property" is to be determined by looking to independent sources such as state law.</u>
  - Court has not been very clear about whether one looks to state law for the definition of property, or only to determine the nature of the claimant's interest, with the characterization whether it is private property being a matter of federal constitutional law.
- ***Eastern Enterprises v. Apfel*** suggests that "private property" for the purposes of the Takings Clause refers to identifiable things or discrete assets taken by the government, but does not apply when the government simply imposes a general liability or tax that can be satisfied out of any source of wealth.